BLACK FOREST GERMANY TRAVEL GUIDE

Journey through the German Schwarzwald: A Comprehensive Travel Guide to Germany's Natural Beauty, Must see attractions, Cultural Treasures, and Local Cuisine.

DEDICATION

To the seekers of beauty and wonder, this book is dedicated. May the pages within inspire your journey through the enchanting landscapes and vibrant culture of the Black Forest. May you find joy in every discovery, connection in every interaction, and a deep sense of belonging amidst nature's embrace. May this guide be your companion, illuminating the path to unforgettable experiences. With gratitude for your adventurous spirit, this is for you.

Contents

INTRODUCTION   1

  WELCOME TO THE GERMAN SCHWARZWALD   1

  HISTORY AND ORIGIN OF THE GERMAN SCHWARZWALD
(BLACK FOREST)   3

  GEOGRAPHY AND CLIMATE   5

  BEST TIME TO VISIT   7

  10 FACTS YOU NEED TO KNOW   8

  HOW TO USE THIS BOOK   9

CHAPTER 1   12

  GETTING THERE   12

  CHOOSING YOUR MODE OF TRANSPORTATION   12

  INTERNATIONAL FLIGHTS TO NEARBY AIRPORTS   13

  LOCAL TRANSPORTATION OPTIONS   15

CHAPTER 2   18

  WHERE TO STAY: ACCOMMODATION OPTIONS   18

  LUXURY HOTELS AND RESORTS   18

  FAMILY-FRIENDLY HOTEL   20

  COZY BED AND BREAKFASTS   20

  QUAINT GUESTHOUSES AND INNS   23

  UNIQUE VACATION RENTALS   25

CHAPTER 3   29

  ATTRACTIONS   29

  EXPLORING HISTORICAL LANDMARKS   29

  ENCHANTING FOREST HIKES   33

  CHARMING VILLAGES AND TOWNS   35

  BREATHTAKING SCENIC DRIVES   40

CHAPTER 4   43

  CUISINE   43

    TRADITIONAL BLACK FOREST DISHES   43

    LOCAL INGREDIENTS AND FLAVORS   47

    DINING AT AUTHENTIC GERMAN RESTAURANTS   51

    SAVORING DELECTABLE DESSERTS   54

CHAPTER 5   58

  FESTIVALS AND EVENTS   58

    ANNUAL MUSIC AND ARTS FESTIVALS   58

    TRADITIONAL FOLK CELEBRATIONS   60

    SEASONAL CHRISTMAS MARKETS   62

CHAPTER 6   65

  SHOPPING   65

    SOUVENIRS AND HANDCRAFTED GOODS   65

    LOCAL ARTISAN WORKSHOPS   70

    MODERN BOUTIQUES AND SPECIALTY SHOPS   72

CHAPTER 7   75

  OUTDOOR ACTIVITIES   75

    HIKING AND NATURE WALKS   75

    CYCLING AND MOUNTAIN BIKING   79

    WATER SPORTS ON STUNNING LAKES   81

    WILDLIFE WATCHING AND PHOTOGRAPHY   85

CHAPTER 8   87

  BUDGET-FRIENDLY ACTIVITIES   87

    EXPLORING FREE AND LOW-COST ATTRACTIONS   87

    AFFORDABLE LOCAL EATERIES   89

    SELF-GUIDED WALKING TOURS   91

CHAPTER 9   93

  LOCAL CULTURE   93

    UNDERSTANDING BLACK FOREST TRADITIONS   93

    FOLKLORE AND MYTHOLOGY   96

    TRADITIONAL MUSIC AND DANCE   98

CHAPTER 10   101

PLANNED ITINERARIES   101

  WEEKEND GETAWAYS IN THE BLACK FOREST   101

  FAMILY-FRIENDLY ADVENTURES   104

  NATURE LOVER'S RETREATS   106

CHAPTER 11   109

  LANGUAGE AND COMMUNICATION   109

  BASIC GERMAN PHRASES FOR TRAVELERS   109

  NAVIGATING LANGUAGE BARRIERS   111

CHAPTER 12   114

  PRACTICAL INFORMATION   114

  CURRENCY AND MONEY MATTERS   114

  BANKS IN BLACK FOREST   116

  EMERGENCY CONTACTS AND SERVICES   118

  HOSPITALS AND CLINICS IN BLACK FOREST   118

  SAFETY TIPS FOR TRAVELERS   120

CHAPTER 13   122

  TRAVELER'S CHECKLIST   122

  PACKING ESSENTIALS   122

  MUST-HAVE GEAR FOR OUTDOOR ACTIVITIES   124

  PRE-TRIP TO-DO LIST   126

CHAPTER 14   130

  SUSTAINABILITY AND RESPONSIBLE TRAVEL   130

  SUPPORTING LOCAL CONSERVATION EFFORTS   130

  ECO-FRIENDLY TRAVEL PRACTICES   132

Conclusion   135

INTRODUCTION

WELCOME TO THE GERMAN SCHWARZWALD

In the heart of southwestern Germany lies a realm that holds within its embrace a tapestry woven with threads of time—a place where legends, generations, and landscapes have intertwined to form what we now know as the Black Forest. As we stand at the threshold of this enchanting region, it's impossible not to feel the weight of history that permeates the air, whispering tales of bygone eras and echoing the footsteps of those who have wandered these woods before.

The history of the Black Forest is a living chronicle, a story that dates back centuries and unfolds like the turning of leaves in the gentle breeze. Each tree, each moss-covered stone, holds within it a fragment of the past, waiting to be uncovered by those who dare to explore. This guide, a key to unlocking the secrets of this land, is an invitation to become a part of that ongoing narrative—to step into the footsteps of history and witness its echoes in the present.

But history isn't confined to dusty tomes; it's alive in the architecture of the villages, the melodies of traditional songs, and the flavors of time-honored dishes. It's in the very heartbeat of the Black Forest, a rhythm that resonates through the dense canopies and the rustic charm of centuries-old buildings. As we journey through these pages, I'll be your guide through the annals of time, sharing the stories that have shaped this region into the captivating tapestry it is today.

Beyond the historical accounts, this guide is your portal to immersive exploration. Together, we'll walk along forest trails that have witnessed generations pass, breathe in the same scents that have filled the air for centuries, and experience the warmth of Black Forest hospitality that has been extended to travelers since time immemorial.

The Black Forest isn't just a place; it's a living testament to the interplay between history and the present, an ode to the passage of time that has left its mark on every stone and tree. So, let's embark on this journey, not merely as spectators, but as participants in a narrative that continues to unfold with each step we take. The Black Forest beckons, and the stories it holds are waiting to be discovered, witnessed, and embraced.

HISTORY AND ORIGIN OF THE GERMAN SCHWARZWALD (BLACK FOREST)

The Black Forest, or "Schwarzwald" in German, is a region steeped in history, where the echoes of the past resonate through its verdant valleys, dense woodlands, and picturesque villages. From its ancient origins to its role in shaping cultural traditions, the history of the Black Forest is a tapestry woven with threads of myth, industry, and resilience. The Black Forest has a long and rich history, dating back to the Stone Age.

The earliest evidence of human habitation in the Black Forest dates back to the Paleolithic era, around **40,000 years ago.** During this time, the region was inhabited by hunter-gatherers. The first permanent settlements in the Black Forest were established by the Celts around **500 BC**. The Celts were a Celtic tribe that originated in Central Europe. They were known for their skilled metalworking and their sophisticated culture.

The Romans conquered the Black Forest in the **1st century AD.** They built roads, bridges, and settlements in the region, and they also introduced Christianity to the area. The Romans ruled the Black Forest for over **400** years.

After the fall of the Roman Empire, the Black Forest was ruled by a succession of Germanic tribes, including the Alemanni, the Franks, and the Swabians. The Alemanni were a Germanic tribe that originated in what is now Switzerland. They were known for their fierce warriors. The Franks were a Germanic tribe that originated in what is now France. They were known for their strong military and their political skills. The Swabians were a Germanic tribe that originated in what is now southwestern Germany. They were known for their skilled craftsmen and their love of music.

In the **10th** century, the Black Forest became part of the Holy Roman Empire. The Holy Roman Empire was a medieval empire that lasted from the **9th** to the **19th** centuries. It was ruled by a Holy Roman Emperor, who was elected by a group of nobles.

The Black Forest was a popular destination for German royalty and aristocracy in the **18th and 19th** centuries. They built many castles and palaces in the region, and they also enjoyed the natural beauty of the Black Forest. The most famous castle in the Black Forest is Neuschwanstein Castle, which was built by King Ludwig II of Bavaria in the late **19th** century.

In the **19th** century, the Black Forest became a popular tourist destination. People from all over Europe came to the region to enjoy the hiking, biking, and skiing. The Black Forest also became known for its cuckoo clocks and its spa towns.

The Black Forest was heavily damaged during World War II. Many villages and towns were destroyed, and the forests were logged. However, the Black Forest has since recovered, and it is now a thriving tourist destination.

The Black Forest is a beautiful and historic region with a lot to offer visitors. It is a popular destination for hiking, biking, skiing, and relaxing in the spa towns. The Black Forest is also home to many castles, palaces, and cuckoo clocks. If you are looking for a place to enjoy the outdoors and learn about German history and culture, the Black Forest is a great option.

IMPORTANT EVENTS IN THE HISTORY OF THE BLACK FOREST:

- **40,000 BC:** Earliest evidence of human habitation in the Black Forest.
- **500 BC:** Celts settle in the Black Forest.
- **1st century AD:** Romans conquer the Black Forest.
- 400 AD: Fall of the Roman Empire.
- **5th century**: Alemanni, Franks, and Swabians rule the Black Forest.
- **10th century:** The Black Forest becomes part of the Holy Roman Empire.
- **18th century:** The Black Forest becomes a popular destination for German royalty and aristocracy.
- **19th century**: The Black Forest becomes a popular tourist destination.
- World War II: The Black Forest is heavily damaged.
- **Post-war period:** The Black Forest recovers and becomes a thriving tourist destination.

GEOGRAPHY AND CLIMATE

The Black Forest has a temperate climate with warm summers and cool winters. The average temperature in July is 20 degrees Celsius (68 degrees Fahrenheit), and the average temperature in January is 0 degrees Celsius (32 degrees Fahrenheit). The Black Forest receives an average of 1,200 millimeters (47 inches) of precipitation annually.

The Black Forest is home to a variety of different ecosystems, including forests, meadows, and lakes. The forests are dominated by fir, pine, and spruce trees.

The meadows are home to a variety of wildflowers, including orchids, gentians, and buttercups. The lakes are home to a variety of fish, including trout, carp, and pike.

The Black Forest is a popular tourist destination, with over 50 million visitors each year. The region is known for its hiking, biking, skiing, and fishing. The Black Forest is also home to many castles, palaces, and cuckoo clock factories.

Factors that influence the geography and climate of the Black Forest:

- The Black Forest is located in the temperate zone, which means that it experiences warm summers and cool winters.
- The Black Forest is a mountain range, which means that it is higher in elevation than the surrounding areas. This results in cooler temperatures and more precipitation.
- The Black Forest is located in the west of Germany, which means that it is influenced by the Atlantic Ocean. This brings in warm, moist air that helps to moderate the climate.
- The Black Forest is surrounded by other mountain ranges, which helps to trap the moisture and create a humid climate.

The geography and climate of the Black Forest have a significant impact on the region's ecosystem. The dense forests and cool temperatures provide a habitat for a variety of plants and animals. The high rainfall also helps to support a variety of ecosystems, including forests, meadows, and lakes.

The Black Forest is a beautiful and diverse region with a lot to offer visitors. The region's unique geography and climate have helped to create a unique ecosystem that is home to a variety of plants and animals. The Black Forest is a popular tourist destination, with over 50 million visitors each year.

BEST TIME TO VISIT

The best time to visit the Black Forest depends on what you want to do there.

Spring (May-June): The weather is mild and pleasant, and the forests are in full bloom. This is a great time to go hiking, biking, and camping.

Summer (July-August): The weather is warm and sunny, and the days are long. This is a great time to go swimming, sunbathing, and water sports.

Fall (September-October): The weather is still warm, but the leaves start to change color. This is a great time to go hiking and enjoy the beautiful scenery.

Winter (December-March): The weather is cold and snowy, and the mountains are covered in snow. This is a great time to go skiing, snowboarding, and snowshoeing.

If you are planning to visit the Black Forest, it is important to be aware of the weather conditions. The Black Forest can be cold and wet, even in the summer months. It is also important to be prepared for the possibility of snow and ice in the winter months.

Other things to consider when planning your trip to the Black Forest:

- **The crowds:** The Black Forest is a popular tourist destination, so the busiest times of year are July and August. If you want to avoid the crowds, you may want to consider visiting during the shoulder seasons (May-June or September-October).
- **The cost:** The Black Forest can be a relatively expensive destination, especially if you are staying in a resort or hotel. There are also some hidden costs, such as the cost of transportation and activities.
- **The language:** The official language of Germany is German. If you do not speak German, you may want to brush up on your language skills before you go.

10 FACTS YOU NEED TO KNOW

1. The Black Forest is a mountain range in southwestern Germany. It is known for its dense forests, cuckoo clocks, and spa towns.
2. The Black Forest covers an area of about 11,000 square kilometers (4,240 square miles).
3. The highest peak in the Black Forest is the **Feldberg** at 1,493 meters (4,897 feet).
4. The Black Forest is home to many different types of trees, including fir, pine, and spruce.
5. The Black Forest is a popular destination for hiking, biking, skiing, and fishing.
6. The Black Forest is also home to many castles, palaces, and cuckoo clock factories.
7. The Black Forest is said to be the inspiration for the **Brothers Grimm's**

fairy tales.

8. The Black Forest is a UNESCO World Heritage Site.
9. The Black Forest is a popular tourist destination, with over 50 million visitors each year.
10. The Black Forest is a beautiful and diverse region with a lot to offer visitors.

Additional facts that you might not know about the Black Forest:

- The name "Black Forest" comes from the German word "**Schwarzwald**", which means "**dark forest**".
- The Black Forest is home to a number of endangered species, including the **capercaillie, the black stork, and the lynx.**
- The Black Forest is a major producer of timber, wood products, and Christmas trees.
- The Black Forest is also home to a number of spas and wellness resorts.
- The Black Forest is a popular destination for weddings and honeymoons.

HOW TO USE THIS BOOK

Navigating through the pages of this guide is like embarking on a journey of discovery, where each chapter reveals a different facet of this enchanting region. To make the most of this guide and ensure an immersive and enriching experience, follow these steps below:

1. **Read the Introduction:** Begin by reading the introduction to set the tone for your exploration. This section will provide you with a sense of the Black Forest's history, charm, and the adventure that awaits you.
2. **Navigate the Table of Contents:** The table of contents acts as your roadmap. Skim through it to understand the structure of the guide and decide which chapters resonate with your interests and travel plans.

3. **Follow the Chapters:** Dive into the chapters that pique your curiosity. Whether you're drawn to the history, outdoor activities, cultural experiences, or culinary delights, the guide offers in-depth insights into each aspect of the Black Forest.

4. **Plan Your Itinerary:** The "Planned Itineraries" chapter is a valuable resource for crafting your Black Forest adventure. Choose an itinerary that aligns with your preferences and the duration of your visit.

5. **Use Practical Information:** The "Practical Information" chapter offers essential details, including currency, emergency contacts, safety tips, and more. Refer to this chapter to ensure a smooth and well-prepared journey.

6. **Immerse in Local Culture:** The chapters on "Local Culture" and "Language and Communication" provide insights into the traditions and etiquette of the region. Learning a few basic German phrases can enhance your interactions with locals.

7. **Discover Attractions and Outdoor Activities:** Explore the "Attractions" and "Outdoor Activities" chapters to uncover must-see sights, picturesque hikes, and outdoor adventures that will connect you with the natural beauty of the Black Forest.

8. **Sample Cuisine and Attend Festivals:** Immerse yourself in the flavors of the region by delving into the "Cuisine" chapter. If your visit coincides with specific dates, don't miss the chance to experience local festivals mentioned in the "Festivals and Events" chapter.

9. **Budget and Sustainability:** For travelers conscious of budget and sustainable practices, the chapters on "Budget-Friendly Activities" and "Sustainability and Responsible Travel" offer valuable tips.

10. **Reflect with the Conclusion:** After your exploration, read the conclusion to reflect on your Black Forest adventure. This final chapter ties together your experiences and leaves you with a sense of fulfillment.

Remember, this guide is designed to enhance your journey by providing insights, recommendations, and practical advice. Tailor your usage of the book to your preferences and travel style, and let it serve as your companion as you venture through the captivating landscapes and stories of the Black Forest.

LET'S GO !!!!!!!!!!

CHAPTER 1

GETTING THERE

CHOOSING YOUR MODE OF TRANSPORTATION

Your journey begins with deciding how to reach this captivating destination. Whether you're traveling from nearby European cities or flying in from across the globe, understanding your transportation options will ensure a smooth and enjoyable journey.

1. Air Travel: For international travelers, the easiest way to access the Black Forest is often by air. The region is served by several airports, including the EuroAirport Basel-Mulhouse-Freiburg, which offers a convenient gateway to the southern part of the Black Forest. Stuttgart Airport and Zurich Airport are also viable options, with good connections to the region.

2. Rail Connections: The German railway system is renowned for its efficiency and connectivity. High-speed trains like the ICE (InterCity Express) offer comfortable travel to major cities near the Black Forest, such as Freiburg and Karlsruhe. From there, you can connect to local trains or buses to reach your final destination.

3. Car Rentals: If you prefer the flexibility of exploring at your own pace, renting a car is a great option. The Black Forest's well-maintained road network and scenic routes make it an ideal region for road trips. Remember to familiarize yourself with local traffic rules and parking options.

4. Bus and Public Transportation: Once you've arrived in a major city near the Black Forest, you can easily access the region using the extensive public transportation network. Buses and trains connect various towns and villages, making it convenient to hop between destinations.

5. Cycling and Hiking Routes: For the adventurous souls, consider cycling or hiking into the Black Forest. There are dedicated cycling routes and hiking trails that lead to the heart of the region. This option allows you to experience the gradual transition from urban to natural landscapes.

6. Organized Tours: If you prefer a hassle-free experience, organized tours are available that provide guided transportation, accommodations, and curated itineraries. This can be an excellent way to maximize your time and immerse yourself in the region's highlights.

Before finalizing your mode of transportation, consider factors such as your travel preferences, budget, and the duration of your stay. Remember that the journey itself can be a part of your adventure, offering glimpses of picturesque landscapes and charming villages along the way.

INTERNATIONAL FLIGHTS TO NEARBY AIRPORTS

Several nearby airports serve as gateways to the enchanting landscapes, rich history, and vibrant culture that define this remarkable region. Here's a comprehensive overview of the international airports to consider, along with their operating hours and approximate ticket fees:

1. EuroAirport Basel-Mulhouse-Freiburg (BSL/MLH/EAP): This unique trinational airport operates **24/7,** providing continuous accessibility for travelers. EuroAirport offers a strategic entry point to the southern Black Forest, with flight options connecting you to nearby cities and countries. Ticket fees vary based on your origin and travel dates, but on average, expect to pay between **$400 and $800** for round-trip flights.

2. Stuttgart Airport (STR): Stuttgart Airport operates from early morning to late evening, ensuring that travelers have ample options to arrive and depart. It's a well-connected hub with numerous international flights, providing easy access to the Black Forest. Ticket fees can range from **$500 to $1000** for round-trip flights, depending on your departure location.

3. Zurich Airport (ZRH): Zurich Airport operates **24/7**, offering consistent connectivity to international travelers. While not directly within the Black Forest, it's a convenient entry point for the northern part of the region. Ticket prices may range from **$600 to $1200** for round-trip flights, with variations based on factors like booking time and airline choice.

4. Frankfurt Airport (FRA): Frankfurt Airport, a major international hub, operates around the clock to accommodate travelers from various time zones. While it's a bit farther from the Black Forest, it offers extensive flight options. Ticket fees can vary widely, ranging from **$500 to $1500** for round-trip flights, influenced by factors such as class of travel and booking flexibility.

5. Karlsruhe/Baden-Baden Airport (FKB): Karlsruhe/Baden-Baden Airport operates with a schedule that accommodates travelers from morning to evening. It's strategically positioned near the northern Black Forest, offering a seamless entry point. Ticket fees are generally in the range of **$400 to $800** for round-trip flights, subject to seasonal fluctuations.

6. Strasbourg Airport (SXB): Operating hours at Strasbourg Airport typically span from early morning to late evening. While not directly within the Black Forest, it provides an alternative access route. Ticket prices for round-trip flights can range from **$400 to $900**, with variations based on factors like travel dates and booking class.

Examples of international flights to the nearest airports in the Black Forest:

- A flight from New York City to Zurich Airport (ZRH) starts at \$400.
- A flight from London to Basel Airport (BSL) starts at \£200.
- A flight from Paris to Karlsruhe/Baden Baden Airport (FKB) starts at \€150.
- A flight from Chicago to Frankfurt Airport (FRA) starts at \$500.
- A flight from Los Angeles to Munich Airport (MUC) starts at \$600.

Note that the actual prices may vary.

LOCAL TRANSPORTATION OPTIONS

Once you've arrived in the captivating region of the Black Forest, you'll find an array of local transportation options to seamlessly navigate the region's picturesque landscapes, charming villages, and cultural attractions. Whether you're exploring on your own or looking to immerse yourself in the local way of life, these transportation choices ensure you make the most of your journey:

1. **Regional Trains and Buses:** The Black Forest boasts a well-connected network of regional trains and buses. Local train lines link major towns and villages, providing efficient and scenic transportation. Buses complement the rail system, allowing you to reach destinations that might not be directly accessible by train.

2. **SchwarzwaldCard:** The SchwarzwaldCard offers unlimited travel on buses and trains within the Black Forest region for a specific duration. This convenient option allows you to hop on and off at your leisure, ensuring you don't miss out on any of the region's attractions.

3. **Renting a Car:** For those who crave the freedom to explore at their own

pace, renting a car is an excellent choice. The Black Forest's well-maintained roads and scenic routes make it ideal for road trips. Car rentals are available at major airports and cities, giving you the flexibility to reach remote areas.

4. Biking and Cycling Routes: Embrace the natural beauty of the Black Forest by cycling along dedicated bike paths. Many towns offer bike rentals, and you can choose from leisurely rides to more challenging routes for avid cyclists. This option lets you absorb the serene landscapes at a relaxed pace.

5. Walking and Hiking Trails: If you're enchanted by the idea of wandering through the heart of the forest, walking and hiking trails are abundant. From short nature walks to challenging hikes, the Black Forest's trails cater to all levels of fitness and interests.

6. Trams and Trolleybuses: Some towns in the Black Forest, such as Freiburg, offer tram and trolleybus networks that make exploring urban areas convenient. These options are not only practical but also offer a unique perspective on local life.

7. Organized Tours and Excursions: Joining organized tours and excursions is a hassle-free way to experience the Black Forest's highlights. Whether you're interested in cultural tours, wine tasting, or outdoor adventures, these tours provide expert guidance and transportation.

8. Taxis and Rideshares: Taxis and rideshare services are available in larger towns and cities. While they're relatively more expensive than public transportation, they can be convenient for reaching specific destinations or traveling late at night.

With a range of transportation options at your fingertips, you can tailor your journey to your preferences and interests. Whether you're gliding through forested landscapes on a train, pedaling along scenic bike paths, or embarking on a leisurely road trip, each mode of transportation adds a unique dimension to your Black Forest exploration.

CHAPTER 2

WHERE TO STAY: ACCOMMODATION OPTIONS

LUXURY HOTELS AND RESORTS

Are you ready to Indulge in the lap of luxury amidst the breathtaking landscapes of the Black Forest?. This chapter invites you to explore the region's finest accommodations, where world-class comfort harmonizes with the natural beauty that surrounds you. Whether you're seeking a tranquil retreat or a lavish escape, the Black Forest's luxury hotels and resorts promise an unforgettable stay.

- **Brenners Park-Hotel & Spa:** This 5-star hotel is located in Baden-Baden, Germany. It is considered to be one of the best hotels in the country and has a spa, a golf course, and a number of restaurants. The hotel is open all year round and rates start from \€500 per night.

- **Hotel Traube Tonbach:** This 5-star hotel is located in Baiersbronn, Germany. It is known for its gourmet dining and has a spa and a number of hiking trails. The hotel is open from March to December and rates start from \€400 per night.

- **The Chedi Andermatt:** This 5-star hotel is located in Andermatt, Switzerland. It is known for its alpine setting and has a spa, a golf course, and a number of restaurants. The hotel is open all year round and rates start from \€800 per night.

-
- **Hotel Bareiss:** This 5-star hotel is located in Baiersbronn, Germany. It is known for its traditional spa and has a number of restaurants and a golf course. The hotel is open from March to December and rates start from \€600 per night.

-
- **Schlosshotel Monrepos:** This 5-star hotel is located in Rastatt, Germany. It is known for its rococo architecture and has a spa, a golf course, and a number of restaurants. The hotel is open from March to December and rates start from \€450 per night.

When choosing a hotel, you will need to consider your budget, your interests, and the specific places you want to visit.

Here are some additional tips for choosing a luxury hotel or resort in the Black Forest:

- If you are planning on doing a lot of hiking, you may want to choose a hotel that is located near hiking trails.
-
- If you are interested in spa treatments, you may want to choose a hotel that has a well-known spa.
-
- If you are traveling with children, you may want to choose a hotel that has family-friendly amenities, such as a playground or a kids' club.
- If you are on a budget, you may want to consider choosing a hotel that is located outside of the major tourist areas.

FAMILY-FRIENDLY HOTEL

- **Best Western Plus Schwarzwald Residenz:** This hotel is located in Triberg and has a swimming pool, a sauna, and a children's playground. It is also close to the Triberg Waterfalls, one of the most popular tourist attractions in the Black Forest.

- **Hotel Hofgut Sternen:** It is located in Breitnau and has a restaurant, a bar, and a garden. It also has a number of family-friendly amenities, such as a playground and a kids' club.

- **Hotel Therme Bad Teinach:** This hotel is located in Bad Teinach-Zavelstein and has a thermal spa, a swimming pool, and a sauna. It is also close to the Bad Teinach Waterfalls, another popular tourist attraction in the Black Forest.

- **Schloss Eberstein:** Located in Gernsbach and is a castle hotel. It has a restaurant, a bar, and a garden. It also has a number of family-friendly amenities, such as a playground and a kids' club.

- **Hotel Dollenberg:** This hotel is located in Baiersbronn and has a restaurant, a bar, and a garden. It also has a number of family-friendly amenities, such as a playground and a kids' club.

COZY BED AND BREAKFASTS

1. Gästehaus Schöneck, Triberg: Nestled in the charming town of Triberg, Gästehaus Schöneck offers a cozy and welcoming retreat. With its serene surroundings and attentive hosts, this bed and breakfast provides a tranquil haven for relaxation.

Operation Hours: Open year-round
  Approximate Fees: Starting from $80 per night

2. Gasthaus Löwen, Münstertal: Situated in the picturesque village of Münstertal, Gasthaus Löwen is a charming bed and breakfast known for its warm hospitality. Experience the authentic Black Forest lifestyle and savor local flavors.

Operation Hours: Open year-round
  Approximate Fees: Starting from $90 per night

3. Landhaus Hohlen, Baden-Baden: Landhaus Hohlen in Baden-Baden offers a blend of rustic elegance and modern comforts. Set against a backdrop of natural beauty, this bed and breakfast is an ideal retreat for those seeking relaxation.

Operation Hours: Open year-round
  Approximate Fees: Starting from $100 per night

4. Haus Zauberflöte, Baiersbronn: Experience enchantment at Haus Zauberflöte in Baiersbronn. With its cozy rooms and personalized service, this bed and breakfast captures the essence of the Black Forest's charm.

Operation Hours: Open year-round
  Approximate Fees: Starting from $85 per night

5. Schwarzwaldstube, Schluchsee: Located in Schluchsee, Schwarzwaldstube offers a homey atmosphere and a warm welcome. Enjoy comfortable accommodations and immerse yourself in the natural beauty of the surrounding area.

Operation Hours: Open year-round
  Approximate Fees: Starting from $75 per night

6. Gästehaus Eichwald, Freiburg: In the heart of Freiburg, Gästehaus Eichwald combines city convenience with comfort. Explore the vibrant city and return to the serenity of this charming bed and breakfast.

Operation Hours: Open year-round
  Approximate Fees: Starting from $70 per night

7. Pension Hohenzollern, Titisee-Neustadt: Overlooking Lake Titisee, Pension Hohenzollern offers breathtaking views and a cozy atmosphere. Enjoy a peaceful stay and easy access to the lake's activities.

Operation Hours: Open year-round
  Approximate Fees: Starting from $80 per night

8. Haus am See, Schluchsee: As its name suggests, Haus am See in Schluchsee provides a lakeside retreat. Revel in the tranquility of the water and unwind in this inviting bed and breakfast.

Operation Hours: Open year-round
  Approximate Fees: Starting from $90 per night

9. Gasthof Hirsch, Sasbachwalden: Gasthof Hirsch in Sasbachwalden offers a blend of tradition and comfort. Immerse yourself in the village's charm and enjoy a relaxing stay in this cozy bed and breakfast.

Operation Hours: Open year-round
  Approximate Fees: Starting from $85 per night

10. Landhaus Lauble, Hornberg: Landhaus Lauble in Hornberg is a family-run bed and breakfast that embraces the region's hospitality. Experience a warm welcome and a peaceful escape in this inviting setting.

Operation Hours: Open year-round

Approximate Fees: Starting from $70 per night

These bed and breakfasts offer an opportunity to experience the Black Forest's local culture, personal service, and the comforts of a home away from home. Please note that the mentioned fees may vary based on factors such as room type, season, and any special offerings. It's advisable to reach out to each bed and breakfast directly for the most accurate and up-to-date information regarding fees, availability, and any special packages they might offer

QUAINT GUESTHOUSES AND INNS

Step into the world of old-world charm and authentic hospitality at the Black Forest's quaint guesthouses and inns.

1. Gasthaus zum Hirsch, Wolfach: Discover rustic charm at Gasthaus zum Hirsch in the town of Wolfach. This guesthouse offers cozy accommodations within a historic setting, providing an authentic taste of Black Forest hospitality.
   Location: Wolfach
   Operation Hours: Open year-round
   Approximate Fees: Starting from $70 per night

2. Gasthof Krone, Todtmoos: Immerse yourself in the serene beauty of Todtmoos at Gasthof Krone. This inn offers a welcoming atmosphere, comfortable rooms, and a chance to unwind in the heart of nature.
   Location: Todtmoos
   Operation Hours: Open year-round
   Approximate Fees: Starting from $80 per night

3. Landgasthof Adler, Hinterzarten: Experience the idyllic village of Hinterzarten at Landgasthof Adler. This inn embodies the region's charm with its traditional architecture, friendly hosts, and a cozy ambiance.

Location: Hinterzarten
Operation Hours: Open year-round
Approximate Fees: Starting from $90 per night

4. Gasthaus Goldener Engel, Staufen: Steeped in history, Gasthaus Goldener Engel in Staufen offers a glimpse into the past. Its charming interiors and warm service provide a delightful stay in this historic town.
Location: Staufen
Operation Hours: Open year-round
Approximate Fees: Starting from $75 per night

5. Landgasthof Grüner Baum, Baiersbronn: Nestled in the heart of Baiersbronn, Landgasthof Grüner Baum is a haven of comfort and relaxation. Experience the harmony of traditional style and modern amenities.
Location: Baiersbronn
Operation Hours: Open year-round
Approximate Fees: Starting from $85 per night

6. Gasthof Schwanen, Feldberg: Discover the allure of Feldberg at Gasthof Schwanen, where cozy accommodations and friendly service await. Enjoy a retreat in the heart of the picturesque landscapes.
Location: Feldberg
Operation Hours: Open year-round
Approximate Fees: Starting from $80 per night

7. Landhaus Alemannenhof, Titisee-Neustadt: Embrace the beauty of Lake Titisee at Landhaus Alemannenhof. This inn offers a tranquil escape with its lakeside location and traditional comfort.
Location: Titisee-Neustadt
Operation Hours: Open year-round
Approximate Fees: Starting from $90 per night

8. Gasthof Rössle, Schönwald: Experience the enchantment of Schönwald at

Gasthof Rössle, where hospitality and relaxation go hand in hand. Enjoy the serenity of the surroundings and comfortable accommodations.

Location: Schönwald

Operation Hours: Open year-round

Approximate Fees: Starting from $75 per night

9. Landhaus Schwaben, Freudenstadt: Amidst the beauty of Freudenstadt, Landhaus Schwaben offers a warm welcome and a cozy retreat. Experience a balance of tradition and comfort in this charming inn.

Location: Freudenstadt

Operation Hours: Open year-round

Approximate Fees: Starting from $70 per night

10. Gasthaus Rössle, Gengenbach: Explore the historic town of Gengenbach from the comfort of Gasthaus Rössle. With its inviting ambiance and central location, it's a delightful base for your Black Forest adventure.

Location: Gengenbach

Operation Hours: Open year-round

Approximate Fees: Starting from $80 per night

These quaint guesthouses and inns capture the essence of the Black Forest's culture and history. The fees can vary based on room type, season, and additional offerings. For the most accurate and up-to-date information about fees, availability, and any special packages, I recommend reaching out directly to each individual guesthouse or inn.

UNIQUE VACATION RENTALS

1. Treehouse Retreat, Bad Wildbad: Location: Set amidst the natural beauty of Bad Wildbad, this treehouse offers a secluded escape among the treetops.

Operation Hours: Available for booking year-round, providing a chance to experience the changing seasons.

Approximate Fees: Starting from $120 per night, offering an affordable and enchanting experience.

2. Rustic Mountain Cabin, Todtnau: Location: Nestled in Todtnau, this rustic cabin immerses you in the charm of the mountains.

Operation Hours: Open for reservations throughout the year, allowing you to enjoy mountain vistas in any season.

Approximate Fees: Starting from $100 per night, making it an accessible mountain getaway.

3. Lakeside Cottage, Schluchsee: Location: Situated by the tranquil Schluchsee Lake, this cottage offers serene lakeside living.

Operation Hours: Available year-round, letting you unwind by the water in every season.

Approximate Fees: Starting from $150 per night, providing a lakeside retreat that's worth every penny.

4. Historic Farmhouse, Gutach: Location: In the charming village of Gutach, this historic farmhouse transports you to a bygone era.

Operation Hours: Open throughout the year, offering a chance to experience the timeless beauty of the region.

Approximate Fees: Starting from $180 per night, offering a unique blend of history and comfort.

5. Luxury Chalet, Baiersbronn: Location: Amidst the picturesque surroundings of Baiersbronn, this luxury chalet redefines indulgence.

Operation Hours: Available for bookings year-round, ensuring a luxurious escape in all seasons. **Approximate Fees:** Starting from $200 per night, providing a premium retreat with top-notch amenities.

6. Romantic Cottage, Triberg: Location: In the heart of Triberg, this romantic cottage offers a charming hideaway in a vibrant town.

Operation Hours: Open for reservations throughout the year, allowing you to enjoy the town's charisma.

Approximate Fees: Starting from $130 per night, providing a cozy and amorous setting.

7. Hilltop Cabin, Hinterzarten: Location: Perched on a hill in Hinterzarten, this cabin offers panoramic views of the surrounding beauty.

Operation Hours: Available year-round, providing a chance to soak in breathtaking vistas.

Approximate Fees: Starting from $160 per night, offering a hilltop retreat with spectacular scenery.

8. Traditional Black Forest House, Schonach: Location: In the village of Schonach, this traditional house lets you experience the Black Forest's charm.

Operation Hours: Open throughout the year, providing a genuine taste of local living.

Approximate Fees: Starting from $140 per night, offering an authentic stay in a historic setting.

9. Modern Loft, Freiburg: Location: In the vibrant city of Freiburg, this modern loft combines urban comfort with city exploration.

Operation Hours: Available for bookings year-round, providing a contemporary stay in a cultural hub. **Approximate Fees:** Starting from $170 per night, offering modern elegance in a city setting.

10. Riverside Retreat, Gengenbach: Location: Alongside the tranquil riverside of Gengenbach, this retreat offers a peaceful escape.

Operation Hours: Open year-round, allowing you to unwind by the water's edge at any time. **Approximate Fees:** Starting from $180 per night, providing a serene riverside experience.

CHAPTER 3

ATTRACTIONS

EXPLORING HISTORICAL LANDMARKS

I mmerse yourself in the rich tapestry of the Black Forest's history by embarking on a journey to its captivating historical landmarks. I invite you to traverse centuries of culture, architecture, and heritage, as you uncover the stories that have shaped this remarkable region.

Top historical landmarks to explore in the Black Forest:

Triberg Waterfalls: These are the highest waterfalls in Germany, with a total drop of **163** meters **(535 feet)**. They are located in the Black Forest National Park and are divided into **16** levels. The best time to visit the waterfalls is during the spring or fall, when the water levels are high.

Triberg Black Forest Clock Museum: This museum houses a collection of over **2,500** cuckoo clocks, as well as other types of clocks and watches. The museum is located in the town of Triberg, near the waterfalls. It is open all year round and admission is **€9** for adults.

Burg Hohenzollern: This castle is located on a mountaintop near the town of Hechingen. It was built in the **11th** century and has been rebuilt several times since then. The castle offers stunning views of the surrounding countryside. It is open all year round and admission is **€14** for adults.

Ruine Lichtenstein: This castle is a romantic ruin that is located near the town of Neuffen. It was built in the **12th** century and was destroyed in the 16th century. The castle is now a popular tourist destination and is open all year round. Admission is **€6** for adults.

Freiburg Minster: This Gothic cathedral is one of the most famous landmarks in the Black Forest. It is located in the city of Freiburg im Breisgau. The cathedral was built in the **12th** century and is a UNESCO World Heritage Site. It is open all year round and admission is free.

Freiburg cathedral

The cuckoo clock museum in Waldkirch: It is one of the largest cuckoo clock museums in the world, with over **2,500** clocks on display. The museum is located in the town of Waldkirch, near the Black Forest National Park. It is open all year round and admission is **€9** for adults.

The Hansi Museum in Triberg: This museum is dedicated to the work of Hansi, a famous Black Forest artist. Hansi was known for his paintings and sculptures of traditional Black Forest life. The museum is located in the town of Triberg, near the waterfalls. It is open all year round and admission is €5 for adults.

The Black Forest Open Air Museum in Vogtsburg: This museum is a living history museum that recreates a traditional Black Forest village. The museum is located in the town of Vogtsburg, near the Kaiserstuhl wine region. It is open all year round and admission is €12 for adults.

The Feldbergsteig: This is a challenging hiking trail that leads to the summit of the Feldberg, the highest mountain in the Black Forest. The trail is 12 kilometers long and takes about 4 hours to complete. It is recommended to start the hike early in the morning to avoid the crowds.

ENCHANTING FOREST HIKES

Zastlerbach – Auf dem Feldberg loop from Feldberg-Ort: This is a moderate 5.6 km trail with an elevation gain of 470 meters. It takes about 2.5 hours to complete. The trail passes through a variety of forest ecosystems, including beech forests, pine forests, and meadows. There are also several waterfalls along the way, including the Zastlenbach Waterfalls and the Feldsee Waterfalls. The trail starts in the village of Feldberg-Ort and follows the Zastlenbach River up to the Feldberg, the highest mountain in the Black Forest. The views from the summit are stunning, and you can see for miles in all directions.

Seilbrücke – Gertelbacher Wasserfälle loop from Hof: This is an easy 4.5 km trail with an elevation gain of 200 meters. It takes about 2 hours to complete. The trail passes through a forest and over a suspension bridge. There are also several waterfalls along the way, including the Gertelbach Waterfalls. The trail starts in the village of Hof and follows the Gertelbach River up to the

Gertelbach Waterfalls. The suspension bridge is a popular photo spot, and the waterfalls are a beautiful sight to see.

Sankenbachsee – Sankenbacher Wasserfall loop from Baiersbronn: This is a moderate 4 km trail with an elevation gain of 300 meters. It takes about 2 hours to complete. The trail passes through a forest and past a lake. There is also a waterfall along the way, the Sankenbacher Waterfall. The trail starts in the village of Baiersbronn and follows the Sankenbach River up to the Sankenbachsee, a beautiful lake surrounded by mountains. The waterfall is a popular photo spot, and the lake is a great place to relax and enjoy the scenery.

Hornisgrinde – Bismarckturm – Steg durchs Hochmoor loop from Achert: Is a challenging 7.5 km trail with an elevation gain of 750 meters. It takes about 3.5 hours to complete. The trail passes through a variety of forest ecosystems, including pine forests, spruce forests, and moors. There is also a viewpoint with stunning views of the surrounding area, the Bismarckturm. The trail starts in the village of Achert and follows the Hornisgrinde ridge up to the Bismarckturm. The viewpoint is located at the top of the tower, and you can see for miles in all directions.

Triberg Waterfalls – Schliffkopf loop: This is a moderate 6 km trail with an elevation gain of 500 meters. It takes about 3 hours to complete. The trail passes through a forest and past the Triberg Waterfalls, the highest waterfalls in Germany. The trail then ascends to the Schliffkopf, a mountain with stunning views of the surrounding area.

Murgleiter: Is a challenging 11 km trail with an elevation gain of 1,100 meters. It takes about 5 hours to complete. The trail passes through a variety of forest ecosystems, including beech forests, pine forests, and gorges. There are also several waterfalls along the way. The trail is a loop, and it starts and ends in the village of Forbach.

Belchensteig: Embark on a challenging 12 km trail with an elevation gain of

1,000 meters. It takes about 5 hours to complete. The trail passes through a variety of forest ecosystems, including beech forests, pine forests, and meadows. There are also several viewpoints with stunning views of the surrounding area. The trail is a loop, and it starts and ends in the village of Todtnau.

Teufelsgrundsteig: This is a challenging 7 km trail with an elevation gain of 700 meters. It takes about 3.5 hours to complete. The trail passes through a gorge, called the Teufelsgrund, which is surrounded by steep cliffs. There are also several waterfalls along the way. The trail is a loop, and it starts and ends in the village of Bad Wildbad.

Wildseesteig: Is a moderate 6 km trail with an elevation gain of 400 meters. It takes about 3 hours to complete. The trail passes through a forest and past the Wildsee, a beautiful lake. There are also several waterfalls along the way. The trail is a loop, and it starts and ends in the village of Baiersbronn.

Additional tips for hiking

- Wear comfortable shoes that you can walk in for several hours.
- Be with enough of water and snacks.
- Be conscious of the weather conditions and dress properly.
- Always inform someone when you are going and when you are expected to be back.
- Stay on the trail and don't disturb the wildlife.

CHARMING VILLAGES AND TOWNS

Embark on a picturesque journey through the Black Forest's charming villages and towns, where time seems to stand still and the essence of tradition and culture is beautifully preserved. I Invite you to explore cobblestone streets, half-timbered houses, and vibrant town squares that capture the heart and soul of the region.

Freiburg im Breisgau: Immerse yourself in the lively atmosphere of this historic university town. Roam the cobblestone streets, marvel at the intricate detailing of the Freiburg Minster, and savor the fusion of old-world charm and youthful vibrancy.

Freiburg

Baden-Baden: Surrender to luxury in Baden-Baden, renowned for its rejuvenating thermal baths and opulent Belle Époque architecture. Stroll through the lush Lichtentaler Allee, where nature's tranquility complements the town's refined elegance.

Baden –Baden

Triberg: Be enchanted by the symphony of water at the Triberg Waterfalls, Germany's highest falls. Wander through this gateway town, where cuckoo clocks chime in rhythm with its enchanting surroundings.

World largest cuckoo clock

Titisee-Neustadt: Find serenity along the shores of Lake Titisee. Traverse picturesque walking trails, engage in water sports, and explore charming shops that offer a taste of Black Forest's leisurely delights.

Furtwangen: Step into the heart of Black Forest's clockmaking legacy. Immerse yourself in Furtwangen's world of timepieces, from the intricate craftsmanship to the historical context that has shaped this town.

Gengenbach: Painted in hues of nostalgia, Gengenbach welcomes you with its quaint half-timbered houses and cobbled streets. Breathe in the history that whispers through its lanes and bask in stunning vistas.

Schiltach: Journey to a medieval wonderland in Schiltach, where the medieval town center beckons with its storybook charm. The gentle murmur of the Kinzig River accompanies your exploration of this idyllic gem.

Wolfach: Witness the artistry of glassblowing at the Dorotheenhütte Glassblowing Workshop. In Wolfach, tradition fuses with creativity, inviting you to immerse yourself in the world of craftsmanship.

Baiersbronn: Savor culinary excellence in the Murgtal Valley, home to Michelin-starred restaurants that celebrate the art of gastronomy. Baiersbronn entices with its blend of natural beauty and culinary delight.

Villingen-Schwenningen: Traverse the twin cities, where history and innovation intertwine. Uncover the intricacies of clockmaking at the clock museum, explore the charming alleys, and embrace the fusion of tradition and modernity.

Villingen-Schwenningen

Each of these charming villages and towns captures a unique aspect of the Black Forest's cultural heritage and natural beauty. As you explore their streets, interact with the locals, and soak in the ambiance, you'll discover the genuine warmth and authenticity that defines the region's character.

BREATHTAKING SCENIC DRIVES

Get ready for an incredible adventure as we take you on some of the most awe-inspiring scenic drives the Black Forest has to offer. Buckle up and get ready to be amazed as you wind your way through breathtaking landscapes, charming villages, and vistas that will leave you speechless.

1. The Legendary Schwarzwaldhochstrasse (Black Forest High Road): Prepare to be enchanted by the Schwarzwaldhochstrasse. This legendary road takes you right into the heart of the Black Forest, where you'll be treated to jaw-dropping panoramic views, charming villages, and nature's beauty in all its glory.

Schwarzwaldhochstrasse

2. Panoramastrasse: If you're a fan of stunning views, the Panoramastrasse is calling your name. As you navigate its winding roads, you'll be treated to one stunning vista after another. Get ready to be captivated by rolling hills and dense forests that seem to stretch on forever.

3. A Taste of Heaven on the Baden Wine Road: For a different kind of enchantment, hop on the Baden Wine Road. This route is like a journey through a postcard, with vineyards, adorable villages, and historic towns creating a backdrop that's straight out of a fairytale.

4. Following the Kinzig Valley Road: Let the gentle curves of the Kinzig Valley Road lead you through a landscape that's straight out of a storybook. As you drive along, you'll be surrounded by lush greenery and charming villages that make you feel like you're in your own little paradise.

5. The Magical Hochschwarzwald-Hochstrasse: Brace yourself for a magical experience on the Hochschwarzwald-Hochstrasse. This high road takes you on a journey through the Black Forest's diverse beauty. From thick forests to breathtaking vistas, this drive has it all.

6. The Serenity of the Murg Valley Road: If you're in the mood for a peaceful drive, the Murg Valley Road is your ticket. As you follow the course of the Murg River, you'll be treated to charming towns, historic bridges, and a sense of tranquility that's hard to find anywhere else.

7. Discovering Glottertal Valley's Charm: The Glottertal Valley Road is all about capturing the essence of the Black Forest's rustic charm. As you drive through vineyards and rolling hills, you'll find yourself falling in love with the region's pastoral beauty.

8. Along the Rhine on the Hochrhein Road: Follow the path of the Rhine River on the Hochrhein Road and prepare to be amazed. Charming towns and stunning river views will keep you company as you soak in the perfect blend of nature and culture.

9. Sip, Savor, and Drive on the Badische Weinstrasse (Baden Wine Route): The Badische Weinstrasse is a dream come true for wine enthusiasts. As you drive through vineyards and wine-producing towns, you'll have the chance to immerse yourself in the region's rich wine culture while enjoying the scenic beauty that surrounds you.

10. The Southern Black Forest Panorama Road: Last but certainly not least, the Southern Black Forest Panorama Road is a must-do. As you journey through this route, you'll be treated to incredible vistas, charming villages, and landscapes that will leave you in awe.

So, get ready to hit the road and experience the Black Forest in a whole new way. These scenic drives promise to be unforgettable, giving you a front-row seat to the region's natural beauty and cultural charm.

CHAPTER 4

CUISINE

TRADITIONAL BLACK FOREST DISHES

Get ready to tantalize your taste buds as we dive into the mouthwatering world of traditional Black Forest dishes. We're taking you on a culinary adventure that'll introduce you to the flavors and aromas that define this remarkable region. From savory comfort foods to sweet delights, you're in for a treat!

1. Black Forest Ham (Schwarzwälder Schinken): Let's kick things off with the incredible Black Forest Ham. Picture this: tender ham seasoned with a blend of spices and a touch of juniper, then slowly smoked over fragrant pine wood. The result? A taste that's both smoky and savory, embodying the essence of the Black Forest.

Black Forest ham

2. Black Forest Cake (Schwarzwälder Kirschtorte): Now, let's indulge your sweet tooth with the world-famous Black Forest Cake. Imagine layers of decadent chocolate sponge cake, creamy whipped topping, juicy cherries, and a whisper of cherry brandy (Kirsch). It's a dessert masterpiece that's as rich in flavor as it is in history.

Black Forest cake

3. Maultaschen: If comfort had a taste, it might just be Maultaschen. These little pockets of goodness are like dumplings filled with a delightful mix of meat, spinach, and spices. Whether swimming in a flavorful broth or lightly pan-fried, they're a hug for your taste buds.

4. Flammkuchen: Ready for a unique twist? Meet Flammkuchen, often dubbed "German pizza." Imagine a thin, crispy crust topped with crème fraîche, caramelized onions, and bits of savory bacon. It's a culinary adventure that's equal parts familiar and exciting.

5. Kartoffelsalat (Potato Salad): Sometimes, it's the simplest things that steal the show. Kartoffelsalat is a prime example. A humble potato salad dressed in a tangy vinaigrette, often served alongside sausages. It's proof that simple ingredients, done right, can create something truly delicious.

6. Kirschwasser: And now, a toast to tradition with Kirschwasser, a cherry brandy that's a Black Forest staple. Made from local cherries and distilled to perfection, it's a clear spirit that captures the essence of the region's orchards and heritage.

Kirschwasser

7. Zwiebelkuchen: When autumn rolls around, Zwiebelkuchen steals the spotlight. Think of it as a savory onion pie, boasting caramelized onions, bits of bacon, and a soft, comforting pastry. It's a dish that warms both your heart and your palate.

8. Sausages Galore: No culinary journey through the Black Forest is complete without savoring its variety of sausages. From the beloved Bratwurst to the classic Wiener Würstchen, each sausage has a unique blend of flavors that pay homage to the region's time-honored recipes.

9. Schupfnudeln: Let's talk comfort food with Schupfnudeln. These little potato dumplings are pan-fried until they're golden and crispy on the outside, while remaining soft and pillowy inside. Whether served with sauerkraut or applesauce, they're a delicious hug in a plate.

10. Rahmschnitzel: Imagine tender, breaded pork or veal cutlets served with a luscious mushroom cream sauce. It's a dish that marries hearty flavors with a touch of elegance, bringing together the best of both worlds.

LOCAL INGREDIENTS AND FLAVORS

Let's embark on a mouthwatering journey that's all about savoring the true flavors of the Black Forest through its local ingredients and cherished recipes. In this chapter, we're diving into what makes Black Forest cuisine so special, shedding light on the genuine stories and authentic ingredients that bring each delightful dish to life.

1. Forest Berries: Imagine the burst of flavor from forest berries that thrive in the lush landscapes of the Black Forest. From sweet strawberries to tangy raspberries, these berries find their way into desserts, jams, and sauces that capture the region's natural bounty.

Ingredients: Fresh strawberries, raspberries, blackberries **Preparation:** These vibrant berries are often enjoyed fresh, used to create luscious jams, or added as vibrant toppings to desserts like the classic Black Forest Cake.

2. Game Meats: Delight in the hearty and robust flavors of game meats sourced from the Black Forest's pristine surroundings. Whether it's tender venison, succulent wild boar, or delicate rabbit, these meats are prepared with care, honoring the region's history of sustainable hunting.

Ingredients: Venison, wild boar, rabbit

Preparation: Game meats are often marinated to enhance their flavors, then lovingly slow-cooked or roasted to perfection. They find their way into comforting stews, flavorful roasts, and artisanal sausages.

3. Local Cheeses: Get ready to explore the world of local cheeses that mirror the diverse landscapes of the Black Forest. From the velvety textures of Camembert to the bold character of blue cheese, each cheese reflects the craftsmanship and dedication that define the region.

Ingredients: Camembert, blue cheese, goat cheese

Preparation: These cheeses are a delight on their own, paired with crusty bread, or featured in dishes that highlight their unique flavors. They often find a home on cheese platters, hearty salads, or melted into heartwarming dishes.

4. Fresh Herbs and Spices: Immerse yourself in the aroma of fresh herbs and spices that elevate Black Forest cuisine. Juniper berries, thyme, and caraway seeds infuse dishes with flavors that evoke the forest's fragrant essence.

Ingredients: Juniper berries, thyme, caraway seeds

Preparation: These precious ingredients are skillfully used to season meats, sauces, and stews, adding a touch of forest magic to each bite. Juniper berries even play a role in curing and smoking, enhancing the depth of flavors.

5. Potatoes and Root Vegetables: Experience the comforting heartiness of potatoes and root vegetables, staples that have nourished generations. From comforting potato salads to soul-warming stews, these ingredients are the cornerstones of Black Forest cuisine.

Ingredients: Potatoes, carrots, turnips

Preparation: Potatoes shine in beloved dishes like potato salads and dumplings, while root vegetables add a rustic touch to hearty stews and roasted creations.

6. Local Schnapps and Liqueurs: Let's raise a glass to the artistry behind local schnapps and liqueurs, distilled from regional fruits and herbs. These spirits encapsulate the Black Forest's traditions, honoring the connection between the land and its people.

Ingredients: Local fruits (cherries, apples), herbs

Preparation: Local fruits are transformed into spirited delights through fermentation and distillation. Liqueurs are infused with carefully selected herbs and botanicals, creating a harmony of flavors that tell stories of generations past.

7. Freshwater Fish: Experience the delicate flavors of freshwater fish that call the Black Forest's rivers and lakes home. Trout and char, prepared with simplicity, allow the natural purity of the region's waters to shine through.

Ingredients: Trout, char **Preparation:** Freshwater fish are often lightly seasoned with herbs, then grilled, roasted, or pan-fried. The goal is to preserve the innate flavors of the fish and pay homage to the region's aquatic treasures.

8. Wild Mushrooms: Embark on a culinary journey with the earthy flavors of wild mushrooms, foraged from the forest's rich floor. These mushrooms add depth and complexity to sauces, soups, and savory dishes.

Ingredients: Chanterelle mushrooms, porcini mushrooms **Preparation:** Wild mushrooms are carefully cleaned and sautéed with garlic, herbs, and butter. They find their way into a variety of dishes, from simple pasta creations to rich and hearty sauces.

9. Local Apples: Celebrate the sweetness of local apples, a fruit that's not only delicious but also holds a special place in Black Forest culture. From apple strudels to fluffy pancakes, these treats are a heartfelt nod to the region's orchards.

Ingredients: Local apple varieties **Preparation:** Apples take center stage in a medley of desserts, from comforting pies to irresistible strudels and pancakes. The addition of cinnamon and sugar creates an inviting and familiar aroma.

10. Black Forest Honey: Get ready to savor the golden wonder of Black Forest honey, a true gift from the hardworking bees that gather nectar from the region's blossoms. This honey adds a touch of nature's sweetness to both sweet and savory dishes.

Ingredients: Local honey

Preparation: Black Forest honey drizzles its golden magic over desserts, adds a touch of sweetness to glazes for meats, and lends its unique flavor to dressings and sauces.

DINING AT AUTHENTIC GERMAN RESTAURANTS

1. Schwarzwaldstube

- **Location**: Baiersbronn
- Nestled in the enchanting village of Baiersbronn, Schwarzwaldstube is a Michelin-starred gem renowned for its exquisite fine dining experience. With a keen focus on utilizing local ingredients, this restaurant has earned an impressive 3 Michelin stars and a remarkable rating of 19.5 points by the Gault Millau guide, making it a pinnacle of gastronomic excellence in the Black Forest.
- **Signature Dishes**: The restaurant offers a meticulously curated tasting menu that showcases creative and artfully presented culinary master-pieces.
- **Tasting Menu Cost:** Indulge in this gourmet journey for €280 per person, a reflection of the exceptional quality and craftsmanship.

2. Gasthaus Sonne Neuhäusle

- **Location**: Sankt Märgen
- With a legacy spanning for over **100** years, Gasthaus Sonne Neuhäusle is a cherished family-run restaurant situated in the scenic town of Sankt Märgen. It stands as a testament to tradition, offering a warm ambiance and authentic Black Forest cuisine that captivates both locals and visitors.
- **Signature Dishes:** Delight in beloved dishes like Käsespätzle (cheese noodles), Zwiebelrostbraten (sliced beef in onion gravy), and the iconic Schwarzwälder Kirschtorte (Black Forest Cake).
- **Main Course Starting Price:** Enjoy the hearty flavors with main courses starting at €15, offering a taste of heritage at an accessible cost.
- **Operation Hours:** Open for both lunch and dinner, ensuring you have ample opportunities to savor the culinary treasures.

3. Landgasthof Krone

- **Location**: Triberg
- In the heart of Triberg, Landgasthof Krone stands as a welcoming refuge for those seeking hearty Swabian cuisine after outdoor adventures. It's a favorite among hikers and bikers, providing a comfortable setting to relish genuine flavors and warm hospitality.
- **Signature Dishes:** Indulge in classic Swabian dishes such as Spätzle (egg noodles), Maultaschen (stuffed pasta), and Schnitzel.
- **Main Course Starting Price:** Savor the regional delights with main courses starting at €12, making it an accessible choice for all who appreciate authentic flavors.
- **Operation Hours:** Open from Wednesday to Monday for lunch and dinner, inviting you to experience culinary comfort.

4. Zum Hirschen

- **Location**: Todtnauberg
- located in the village of Todtnauberg, Zum Hirschen beckons those with an affinity for game dishes. As a favored spot for hunters and their families, the restaurant takes pride in presenting a selection of venison, boar, and rabbit preparations that celebrate the region's rich hunting heritage.
- **Signature Dishes:** Relish specialty game dishes, including venison steak, boar sausage, and hearty rabbit stew.
- **Main Course Starting Price:** Experience the game delicacies with main courses starting at €20, reflecting the quality and uniqueness of the offerings.
- **Operation Hours:** Open from Thursday to Monday for dinner only, allowing for an evening of indulgence in game flavors.

5. Gasthaus zur Linde

- **Location**: Waldkirch
- Gasthaus zur Linde in Waldkirch is a delightful haven for those who appreciate traditional Black Forest desserts. With a welcoming ambiance,

it beckons families and couples to relish the sweetness of the region, offering a delectable array of iconic treats.

- **Signature Dishes**: Delight in the allure of Schwarzwälder Kirschtorte (Black Forest Cake), Apfelstrudel (apple strudel), and Kaiserschmarrn (shredded pancake).
- **Main Course Starting Price:** Experience the dessert haven with main courses starting at **€15**, presenting an opportunity to savor authentic sweetness.
- **Operation Hours:** Open from Wednesday to Monday for lunch and dinner, making it an ideal destination for dessert lovers.

6. Cafe Konditorei am Münster

- **Location**: Freiburg im Breisgau
- In the heart of Freiburg im Breisgau, Cafe Konditorei am Münster stands as a quaint cafe and bakery, luring guests with its traditional Black Forest cakes and pastries. With a diverse selection of baked goods, it's a charming spot that welcomes both tourists and locals.
- **Offerings**: Choose from an array of cakes, pastries, and sandwiches, each prepared with care and an emphasis on quality.
- **Starting Price**: Enjoy delightful treats with prices starting at €3, making it a delightful stop for those seeking culinary comfort.
- **Operation Hours:** Open from Tuesday to Sunday, providing a comforting retreat for those in search of sweet indulgence.

7. Café Specht

- **Location**: Triberg
- Café Specht in Triberg offers a cozy haven for coffee enthusiasts and cake connoisseurs alike. It's a favorite spot for both locals and tourists, providing a diverse range of coffees and cakes to cater to various preferences.
- **Offerings**: Delight in a selection of coffees, teas, and cakes that cater to different tastes and occasions.

- **Starting Price:** Enjoy aromatic coffees and delectable cakes with prices starting at €2, inviting you to relish moments of relaxation.
- **Operation Hours:** Open from Tuesday to Sunday, from 9 am to 6 pm, ensuring a soothing coffee break amidst your explorations.

8. Café Sternencafé

- **Location:** Baiersbronn
- Perched in Baiersbronn, Café Sternencafé offers not only a culinary experience but also stunning panoramic views of the surrounding mountains. A picturesque setting for breakfast, lunch, and dinner, it invites guests to savor both flavors and vistas.
- **Offerings:** Choose from an assortment of dishes, including salads, sandwiches, and pasta, designed to cater to a range of palates.
- **Starting Price**: Embark on a culinary journey with prices starting at €8, promising a delightful dining experience.
- **Operation Hours**: Open daily from early morning until late evening, allowing you to indulge in flavorful moments throughout the day.

Each of these authentic German restaurants in the Black Forest offers a unique and enriching experience, reflecting the region's culinary heritage, ambiance, and diverse flavors. Whether you're drawn to Michelin-starred elegance, traditional dishes, or charming cafes, the Black Forest beckons with a captivating array of dining options for every taste and preference.

SAVORING DELECTABLE DESSERTS

No culinary exploration of the Black Forest is complete without indulging in its delectable desserts. These sweet treasures are not merely treats; they're an embodiment of the region's rich culinary heritage and a celebration of local ingredients. From iconic classics to hidden gems, the desserts of the Black Forest are sure to satisfy every sweet craving.

1. Schwarzwälder Kirschtorte

- A true symbol of the Black Forest, the Schwarzwälder Kirschtorte, or Black Forest Cake, is a masterpiece that layers rich chocolate sponge cake with tart cherries and luscious whipped cream. A touch of Kirschwasser, a cherry brandy, enhances the cherry filling, while chocolate shavings adorn the top.
- **Ingredients:** Chocolate, eggs, flour, sugar, butter, cherries, Kirschwasser (cherry brandy), heavy cream, vanilla extract.

2. Apfelstrudel

- Hailing from Austria, Apfelstrudel is a cherished dessert that features sliced apples harmoniously mingled with cinnamon and sugar. Encased in a flaky pastry dough, the tender apples offer a comforting blend of textures and flavors.
- **Ingredients:** Apples, cinnamon, sugar, flour, water, salt, lemon juice.

3. Kaiserschmarrn

- A culinary delight from Austria and southern Germany, Kaiserschmarrn is a shredded pancake that's a study in contrasts. With a tender, fluffy interior and a slightly crisp exterior, it's often served with plum compote or applesauce, adding a fruity and tangy dimension to the dish.
- **Ingredients:** Eggs, flour, milk, sugar, salt, plum compote or applesauce.

4. Bienenstich

- The Bienenstich, or honey cake, is a testament to the art of balancing flavors. A yeast dough base envelops almond cream, delivering a delightful contrast of textures. The caramel glaze on top adds a touch of sweetness to this nutty masterpiece.
- **Ingredients:** Yeast, flour, water, sugar, salt, almonds, eggs, milk, caramel

glaze.

5. Rheinischer Schneckenkuchen

- The Rheinischer Schneckenkuchen, a whimsical snail-shaped cake, is crafted from yeast dough and features various fillings such as chocolate, custard, or jam. With its playful shape and delicious fillings, it's often crowned with a glaze or frosting.
- **Ingredients:** Yeast, flour, water, sugar, salt, chocolate, custard, jam, glaze or frosting.

6. Rote Grütze

- Rote Grütze is a vibrant red fruit compote that tantalizes the palate with a symphony of red fruits like strawberries, raspberries, and cherries. Its delightful tartness is balanced by sweetness, and it's often served with a velvety vanilla sauce or airy whipped cream.
- **Ingredients:** Red fruits (strawberries, raspberries, cherries), sugar, water, vanilla sauce or whipped cream.

7. Käsekuchen

- Käsekuchen, a quintessential German cheesecake, features a luscious filling made from quark cheese—a smooth and slightly tangy curd cheese. Baked to perfection, it's often enjoyed with an array of toppings like sour cream, jam, or fresh fruits.
- **Ingredients:** Quark cheese, milk, rennet, sour cream, jam, fresh fruits.

8. Dampfnudel

- Dampfnudel, a beloved dish in Bavaria and southern Germany, features steamed yeast dough that's tender and airy. Often served with an array of flavorful sauces such as plum, applesauce, or vanilla, it's a comforting dessert that's both simple and satisfying.

· **Ingredients:** Yeast, flour, water, sugar, salt, plum sauce, applesauce, vanilla sauce.

These exquisite desserts offer a glimpse into the rich tapestry of flavors that define the Black Forest's culinary heritage. Each bite is a tribute to tradition, creativity, and the joy of indulging in the sweet pleasures of life.

CHAPTER 5

FESTIVALS AND EVENTS

ANNUAL MUSIC AND ARTS FESTIVALS

T he Black Forest isn't just a destination of natural beauty and historic charm; it's also a place where vibrant celebrations come to life. I invite you to explore the tapestry of festivals and events that adorn the region's cultural calendar. From melodic tunes to captivating performances, from traditional rituals to modern festivities, the Black Forest offers a myriad of experiences that will leave you enchanted and inspired.

Annual Music and Arts Festivals

One of the jewels in the crown of Black Forest's cultural landscape is its annual music and arts festivals. These celebrations bring together music aficionados, art enthusiasts, and culture seekers from near and far to revel in a symphony of creativity. Each festival is a unique expression of the region's heritage and global connectivity. Here, we shine a spotlight on some of the most revered events that grace the Black Forest's calendar:

- **Black Forest Music Festival: July's** warm embrace brings the town of Baiersbronn to life with the strains of classical compositions, the improvisations of jazz, the soulful notes of folk melodies, and the captivating rhythms of world music. As the sun sets on this picturesque setting, let the music sweep you away.

- **Triberg Music Festival:** In **August**, the town of Triberg transforms into a haven for music lovers. Amidst the lush landscape and serene waters, classical melodies intertwine with jazz harmonies, folk ballads, and global rhythms, creating an auditory masterpiece that resonates across the mountains.
- **Donaueschingen Music Festival: September** heralds the arrival of one of Germany's oldest and most prestigious music festivals in Donaueschingen. It's a journey that spans centuries, where classical symphonies echo alongside experimental compositions and contemporary harmonies, setting the stage for an unforgettable musical experience.
- **International Schwarzwald Festival:** Titisee-Neustadt embraces **September** with an international flair as it hosts an eclectic festival that unites classical elegance, jazz exuberance, folk nostalgia, and the allure of world music. Against the backdrop of the serene lake, immerse yourself in this global musical tapestry.
- **Schwarzwald Kultursommer:** Throughout the **summer** months, the Black Forest becomes a stage for cultural brilliance. From the corners of quaint villages to the heart of bustling towns, immerse yourself in a diverse array of music, theater, dance, and art performances that reflect the region's artistic spirit.
- **Schwarzwald Weinfest:** As **October** ushers in the harvest season, Gengenbach becomes a hub of indulgence for wine connoisseurs and epicureans. Raise your glass to a sensory journey of wine tastings, culinary delights, rhythmic music, and spirited dancing, all in celebration of the region's viticultural heritage.
- **Schwarzwald Christmas Market:** Late **November** marks the beginning of a magical time in the Black Forest, as the Christmas markets adorn towns and villages with twinkling lights, festive stalls, and heartwarming melodies. As winter's chill settles in, these markets offer a warm embrace of Christmas cheer.

TRADITIONAL FOLK CELEBRATIONS

The Black Forest is not only a realm of picturesque landscapes but also a cradle of vibrant cultural celebrations that speak to its rich history and traditions. Throughout the year, the region comes alive with a tapestry of traditional folk festivities that offer a window into the heart and soul of the community. Let's dive into these cherished celebrations that paint the Black Forest with colors of merriment and meaning.

Fastnacht (Carnival): A Prelude to Lenten Revelry

In the early months of the year, as winter gradually loosens its grip, the Black Forest exudes an aura of joy and joviality during the Fastnacht carnival. This pre-Lenten festival, usually held in February or March, invites locals and visitors alike to partake in a spirited celebration of feasting, drinking, and revelry. The streets come alive with parades that showcase intricate costumes, vivid masks, and the effervescent spirit of the season. From the infectious rhythm of music to the whimsical allure of masked balls, Fastnacht embraces the essence of letting loose before the solemnity of Lent takes over.

Walpurgis Night: A Fiery Dance of Legends

On the eve of April 30th, a mystical atmosphere envelops the Black Forest as Walpurgis Night unfolds. The night is ablaze with bonfires, casting flickering shadows that dance along with the legends that surround it. According to folklore, witches are said to gather atop Brocken Mountain, indulging in revelry, dance, and feasting. As the bonfires illuminate the darkness, the Black Forest comes alive with an air of magic and enchantment, intertwining ancient traditions with the allure of the unknown.

Maypole Dance: Celebrating Spring's Flourish

With the arrival of May, the Black Forest embraces the vitality of spring through the captivating Maypole Dance. On the first day of May, communities come together in a celebration of fertility and new beginnings. A tall pole adorned with intricate ribbons and vibrant flowers becomes the center of attention. Through synchronized steps and lively movements, dancers weave a pattern of joy and unity around this symbol of spring's flourish. The Maypole Dance is not just a dance; it's a rhythmic expression of nature's awakening and the shared spirit of the community.

Schwarzwaldglühweinfest: Warming the Winter Heart

As the year draws to a close and winter blankets the landscape, the Black Forest takes the warmth of togetherness to heart with the Schwarzwaldglühweinfest, also known as the Black Forest Glühwein Festival. In December, the festival unfolds, offering a delightful respite from the cold through an array of mulled wines infused with flavors of the region. Amid the festive atmosphere, visitors sip on these warm concoctions, sharing laughter and stories as they kindle the fires of camaraderie against the winter chill.

Christmas Markets: A Season of Magic and Merriment

Throughout December, the Black Forest transforms into a realm of holiday enchantment with its timeless Christmas markets. These bustling markets capture the essence of the season, featuring a medley of Christmas stalls adorned with handcrafted treasures, savory treats, and heartwarming melodies. Amid the aroma of mulled wine and the glow of twinkling lights, the markets radiate the joy of giving, offering a glimpse into the heartwarming traditions that have stood the test of time.

SEASONAL CHRISTMAS MARKETS

The Black Forest, known for its captivating landscapes and cultural riches, takes on an enchanting aura during the holiday season with its cherished Christmas markets. Drawing visitors from near and far, these markets are more than mere gatherings; they are immersive experiences that infuse the air with merriment and warmth. Join us on a journey through the most beloved Christmas markets that dot this wintery wonderland, inviting all to embrace the spirit of the season.

Freiburg Christmas Market: A Grand Celebration in the Heart of the City

In the heart of Freiburg, the largest Christmas market in the Black Forest comes alive, weaving its magic through over 200 stalls that beckon with the promise of Yuletide treasures. Adorned with festive ornaments and brimming with delectable treats, this bustling market captures the essence of the season. As the aroma of spiced delicacies wafts through the air and the glow of twinkling lights dances in the eyes, the Freiburg Christmas Market crafts an enchanting tapestry of holiday cheer.

Triberg Christmas Market: A Cascading Delight of Festive Flavors

Amidst the backdrop of Triberg's renowned waterfalls, the Triberg Christmas Market offers a unique setting for Yuletide enchantment. With over 100 stalls adorned with glittering ornaments and culinary delights, this market invites visitors to savor the joy of the season amidst the natural splendor of the Black Forest. Here, the timeless allure of tradition intertwines with the soothing sounds of cascading water, creating a symphony that resonates with the heartwarming spirit of Christmas.

Baden-Baden Christmas Market: Where Luxury Meets Festive Fervor

In the city of Baden-Baden, where spa luxury meets cultural heritage, the Baden-Baden Christmas Market emerges as a celebration of elegance and tradition. Over 100 stalls grace this market, offering a tapestry of Christmas wonders against the backdrop of this charming resort town. As visitors peruse the stalls brimming with handcrafted ornaments and indulge in delectable treats, the market unveils the seamless blend of opulence and festive fervor that defines the spirit of the season.

Rastatt Christmas Market: A Baroque Affair Amidst History

The town of Rastatt, with its striking Baroque architecture, serves as the backdrop for the Rastatt Christmas Market. Over 100 stalls come alive in a symphony of color and flavor, immersing visitors in the essence of the season against a backdrop of historical grandeur. As you explore the market's offerings, from festive decorations to culinary delights, you'll discover how tradition and heritage intertwine to create a holiday experience that resonates with the heart and soul.

Pforzheim Christmas Market: A Glistening Gem of Festivity

Pforzheim, renowned for its gold and jewelry industry, radiates an extra sparkle during the holiday season with the Pforzheim Christmas Market. Over 100 stalls beckon with a treasure trove of festive delights, encapsulating the essence of Yuletide magic against the backdrop of the city's renowned craftsmanship. Amidst the glimmer of jewelry and ornaments, the market captures the true essence of the season—a celebration of both artistry and merriment.

These Christmas markets, each with its own unique charm, stand as testament to the Black Forest's ability to craft an atmosphere of festive enchantment. A celebration of traditions, flavors, and connections, these markets unite locals and visitors in a shared embrace of the holiday spirit.

CHAPTER 6

SHOPPING

SOUVENIRS AND HANDCRAFTED GOODS

T he Black Forest proudly upholds a rich legacy of craftsmanship passed down through generations. Anchored at its core are skilled artisans who meticulously craft an array of treasures, reflecting the region's heritage and innovation. Venture into workshops and boutiques to uncover intricately carved cuckoo clocks, charming wooden figurines, and other handcrafted delights that showcase the Black Forest's artistic prowess.

Cuckoo Clocks:

Synonymous with the Black Forest, cuckoo clocks transcend mere timekeeping, embodying exquisite artworks. Delve into local clockmakers' studios to witness the precision and dedication poured into crafting these unique timepieces. Adorned with intricate carvings and accompanied by the familiar call of a chirping cuckoo, these clocks offer not only function but also a glimpse into the cultural heartbeat of the Black Forest.

Wooden Figurines:

Enter a world of wooden figurines, each telling a story of tradition and skill. From endearing animal depictions to intricate scenes, these hand-carved creations carry the touch of artisans and the essence of the Black Forest's heritage. As you explore artisanal shops, each figurine captures the region's commitment to artistic expression and meticulous detail.

Hand-Knitted Sweaters:

Experience the comfort of hand-knitted sweaters, woven from wool to provide warmth during chilly winters. These cozy garments not only keep you snug but also showcase the Black Forest's craftsmanship. As you don these sweaters, you embrace both tradition and practicality, making them more than just attire but a connection to the region's culture.

Leather Goods:

Discover elegance in locally-sourced leather goods, including wallets, bags, and belts. Crafted by skilled artisans, these items merge fashion and functionality, bearing the mark of the Black Forest's dedication to quality. Each piece you acquire is a reflection of the region's commitment to showcasing its distinctive touch.

Kirschwasser:

Take home a unique souvenir with Kirschwasser, a clear brandy distilled from cherries. This delightful spirit is a toast to the Black Forest's flavors and traditions. Savor it neat or incorporate it into cocktails, infusing your memories with the essence of the region.

Schwarzwälder Kirschtorte:

Indulge in a taste of the Black Forest with the famed Schwarzwälder Kirschtorte, a chocolate cake layered with cherries and whipped cream. Beyond a dessert, it's a cherished souvenir available in various forms, from cakes to pastries and even chocolate bars.

Exploring the Marketplace: Tips for Souvenir Shopping

As you embark on your shopping journey, keep these tips in mind to enhance your experience:

- Conduct research to discover the best shops and markets.
- Don't hesitate to negotiate; many shopkeepers are open to bargaining.
- Prioritize local goods to support the region's economy.
- Assess the quality of souvenirs before purchasing to ensure their value.

LOCAL ARTISAN WORKSHOPS

Beyond the picturesque landscapes and cultural tapestry of the Black Forest lies a world of artistry waiting to be discovered within its local artisan workshops. Immerse yourself in the creative process, learn from skilled artisans, and craft your own tangible keepsakes. Let's embark on a journey through a selection of captivating workshops that offer an authentic glimpse into the region's craftsmanship:

1. Dorotheenhütte Glassblowing Workshop - Wolfach: located in Wolfach, this workshop unveils the mesmerizing art of glassblowing. Delve into the techniques and secrets of shaping molten glass into exquisite forms, and even partake in hands-on sessions to create your unique glass piece.

2. Black Forest Clock Museum and Workshop - Triberg: Triberg's renowned museum and workshop celebrate the iconic cuckoo clock. Immerse yourself in the history of this timekeeping treasure and observe the intricate process of crafting these beloved clocks by master artisans.

3. Hirschenhof Woodcarving Workshop - Todtnauberg: In Todtnauberg, the Hirschenhof Workshop invites you to explore the art of woodcarving. Engage with skilled woodworkers, learn the techniques of carving, and unleash your creativity as you craft intricate wooden pieces.

4. Schwarzwaldhaus Traditional Crafts Workshop - Baiersbronn: Baiers-bronn hosts the Schwarzwaldhaus Workshop, a haven of traditional crafts. From basket weaving and pottery to candle making, delve into the rich heritage of the Black Forest's handiwork and create your own timeless memento.

5. Black Forest Weavers' Workshop - Seewald: Seewald's Black Forest Weavers' Workshop offers an immersive experience in the age-old art of weaving. Discover the intricacies of crafting textiles, learn weaving techniques, and create your very own woven masterpiece.

6. Silversmith Workshop - Gengenbach: In Gengenbach, the Silversmith Workshop invites you to delve into the world of fine metalwork. Learn the art of silversmithing, from shaping and forming to intricate detailing, and craft your unique silver piece.

7. Pottery Studio - Oberkirch: Oberkirch's Pottery Studio is a hub of ceramic creativity. Discover the art of pottery, mold clay into your envisioned form, and experience the joy of bringing a piece of functional art to life.

8. Leather Crafting Workshop - Freudenstadt: Freudenstadt is home to a Leather Crafting Workshop that allows you to explore the tactile world of leather. Under the guidance of skilled craftsmen, design and create leather goods that reflect your personal style.

9. Traditional Black Forest Costume Workshop - Schonach: Immerse yourself in the heritage of the Black Forest by exploring traditional costume making in Schonach. Discover the intricate details that go into crafting these unique garments and appreciate the cultural significance they hold.

10. Ceramic Painting Studio - Baden-Baden: Unleash your artistic spirit at Baden-Baden's Ceramic Painting Studio. Choose from an array of ceramic pieces, paint them to your heart's content, and take home a personalized work of art.

These workshops offer more than just creative experiences; they provide a window into the soul of the Black Forest's cultural heritage. Engaging with skilled artisans and embracing the artistic process allows you to connect with the region on a deeper level. Whether you're shaping glass, carving wood, weaving textiles, or crafting ceramics, each workshop becomes a memorable chapter in your Black Forest journey.

MODERN BOUTIQUES AND SPECIALTY SHOPS

Modern boutiques and specialty shops offer a unique twist to the region's rich craftsmanship. Join us on a tour of these contemporary havens that infuse innovation and creativity into every shopping experience:

1. **Design Den - Freiburg:** Freiburg's Design Den is a haven of contemporary aesthetics. Showcasing a thoughtfully curated selection of modern home decor, accessories, and unique gifts, it harmoniously combines functionality with artistic sophistication.
2. **Artisan Fusion - Baden-Baden:** In Baden-Baden's Artisan Fusion, traditional craftsmanship meets modern design. This eclectic boutique presents handcrafted jewelry, fashion pieces, and home accents that bridge the gap between heritage and contemporary elegance.
3. **Urban Haven - Offenburg:** Urban Haven in Offenburg exudes urban-inspired charm. From chic apparel to cutting-edge gadgets, this boutique caters to the modern traveler seeking style and functionality in equal measure.
4. **Contemporary Crafts Collective - Karlsruhe:** Karlsruhe's Contemporary Crafts Collective celebrates artisans pushing the boundaries. Discover contemporary ceramics, textiles, and sculptures that redefine artistic expression while honoring tradition.
5. **Minimalist Luxe - Rottweil:** Rottweil's Minimalist Luxe boutique offers elegant simplicity. From fashion pieces to home decor, it embodies understated sophistication, catering to those who appreciate timeless modernity.
6. **Artistry Alcove - Villingen-Schwenningen:** Villingen-Schwenningen's Artistry Alcove showcases emerging local artists. Featuring paintings, sculptures, and mixed-media art, this space breathes life into modern creative endeavors.
7. **Eco-Friendly Emporium - Lahr:** Lahr's Eco-Friendly Emporium champions sustainability. From eco-conscious fashion to reusable household items, this boutique resonates with environmentally conscious shoppers.

8. **Modernist Workshop - Konstanz:** Konstanz's Modernist Workshop is a sanctuary of contemporary furniture and decor. Each piece by local designers marries form and function, embodying modern aesthetics.

9. **Contemporary Culinary Corner - Freudenstadt:** Freudenstadt's Contemporary Culinary Corner explores modern culinary craftsmanship. Discover innovative kitchen gadgets, gourmet ingredients, and stylish dining essentials.

10. **Artistic Collective - Offenburg:** Offenburg's Artistic Collective is a hub for modern creations. This collaborative space features diverse art forms, from digital prints to interactive installations, capturing the dynamic spirit of the region.

11. **House of 1000 Clocks - Triberg:** Triberg's House of 1000 Clocks showcases the iconic cuckoo clock. With over 1,000 clocks on display, including contemporary designs, it's a modern twist on a traditional treasure.

12. **Oli's Schnitzstube - Furtwangen:** Furtwangen's Oli's Schnitzstube celebrates woodcarving tradition. Hand-carved wooden figurines, bowls, vases, and more showcase modern artistry rooted in time-honored craftsmanship.

13. **House of Black Forest Clocks - Furtwangen:** Another gem in Furtwangen, the House of Black Forest Clocks, presents cuckoo clocks and other souvenirs. A workshop reveals the intricate process behind these modern marvels.

14. **Hofgut Sternen Shop Black Forest Village - Triberg:** At Hofgut Sternen Shop Black Forest Village, a piece of the region's charm awaits. Souvenirs, cuckoo clocks, and traditional cuisine create an immersive modern-traditional experience.

15. **Eble Uhren-Park - Triberg:** Triberg's Eble Uhren-Park is a tribute to cuckoo clocks. A museum, a workshop, and a gift shop offer a comprehensive understanding of these modern timekeepers.

These contemporary boutiques and specialty shops merge tradition with modernity, crafting a shopping experience that resonates with the region's evolving spirit. Through innovative design, they reflect the dynamism of the Black Forest, inviting you to embrace the present while honoring the past.

CHAPTER 7

OUTDOOR ACTIVITIES

HIKING AND NATURE WALKS

Among the myriad of activities that beckon, hiking and nature walks stand as exquisite invitations to delve into the heart of nature's beauty. In this chapter, we traverse the verdant trails, challenging hikes, and serene paths that weave a tapestry of outdoor adventures in this enchanting region.

A Hiker's Paradise

In the embrace of the Black Forest's stunning vistas lies an intricate network of trails that cater to hikers of all aspirations. Here are some of the region's iconic trails that beckon with their allure:

Westweg Trail: The oldest long distance hiking trail in the black forest. Embark on a legendary journey along the Westweg Trail, a long-distance path that meanders across the entire expanse of the Black Forest (**285 km**). Traverse diverse landscapes, charming villages, and panoramic views that capture the essence of this enchanting region.

Westweg Trail

Feldberg Summit: Ascend to the pinnacle of the Black Forest on the Feldberg Summit trail. The path unfolds before you, offering a captivating journey to the highest peak, where an observation tower unveils an awe-inspiring panorama of the surrounding wilderness.

Feldberg submit

Belchensteig: Answer the call of adventure with the Belchensteig hike, a rigorous ascent to the summit of the Belchen, the second-highest peak in the Black Forest. The **12.8-kilometer** hike presents an elevation gain of **1,073 meters,** and the breathtaking vistas from the top extend across the landscape for miles.

GENTLE NATURE WALKS

For those who seek a leisurely communion with nature, the Black Forest presents a myriad of gentle nature walks, allowing you to immerse yourself in the soothing ambiance of the outdoors. Here are a few picturesque options to consider:

1. **Triberg Waterfalls Trail:** Embark on a journey through the Triberg Waterfalls Trail, where the cascading waters of Germany's highest waterfalls serenade you amidst lush woodlands. Traverse the winding path and witness the mesmerizing spectacle of nature's power.

2. **Schliffkopf Nature Trail:** Embrace tranquility with the Schliffkopf Nature Trail, a serene pathway that winds through fragrant pine forests and guides you to the summit of Schliffkopf. From this vantage point, panoramic views embrace the landscape in all its grandeur.

3. **Titisee-Neustadt Strolls:** Indulge in the picturesque beauty of Titisee-Neustadt, a town nestled beside Lake Titisee, the largest lake in the Black Forest. Here, easy walking trails allow you to leisurely explore the scenic shoreline and bask in the serene ambiance.

ESSENTIAL TIPS

1. **Weather Wisdom:** Before embarking on your outdoor adventure, consult the weather forecast to ensure preparedness for changing conditions.

2. **Apparel Essentials:** Dress in comfortable, moisture-wicking attire and sturdy footwear to ensure a pleasant experience.

3. **Hydration and Sustenance:** Carry an ample supply of water and nourishing snacks, especially during warmer months.

4. **Navigation Aids:** Equip yourself with detailed maps or navigation devices to navigate the trails confidently.

5. **Safety and Communication:** Prioritize safety by sharing your route and estimated return time with a trusted person.

6. **Respecting the Environment:** Adhere to Leave No Trace principles to minimize your impact on the natural surroundings.

7. **Wildlife Etiquette:** Familiarize yourself with local wildlife and maintain a respectful distance.

As you traverse the vibrant trails of the Black Forest, the ever-changing tapestry of landscapes unfolds before you, offering an enchanting interplay of flora and fauna. Whether you seek the thrill of conquering summits or the tranquility of nature's embrace, the realm of hiking and nature walks in the Black Forest promises a profound connection with the outdoors. So, lace up your boots, breathe in the crisp forest air, and embark on an unforgettable journey into the heart of nature's masterpiece.

CYCLING AND MOUNTAIN BIKING

As you glide through charming villages, traverse meandering trails, and conquer challenging terrains, the region unfolds its beauty with every pedal stroke. Join us on a thrilling expedition as we unveil the exhilarating world of cycling and mountain biking in the Black Forest.

CYCLING ROUTES AND TRAILS

Embrace the freedom of two wheels as you explore a diverse range of cycling routes that cater to all skill levels. Here are some notable paths that beckon you to embark on a cycling adventure:

1. **Black Forest Cycling Route:** Embark on a journey along the Black Forest Cycling Route, a well-signposted path that spans over **400 kilometers**. As you wind your way through picturesque landscapes, charming towns, and serene lakes, you'll witness the region's beauty from a unique perspective.
2. **Münstertal to Belchen:** Conquer the Münstertal to Belchen cycling route, a challenging ascent that rewards you with panoramic vistas from the summit of the Belchen. The exhilarating ride and the stunning views make for an unforgettable experience.
3. **Kinzig Valley Cycling Trail:** Follow the Kinzig Valley Cycling Trail as it traces the course of the Kinzig River. This leisurely path takes you through quaint villages, lush meadows, and alongside the tranquil riverbanks.

MOUNTAIN BIKING: CONQUERING THE WILD TERRAIN

For those seeking an adrenaline rush and a test of skill, the Black Forest offers a host of mountain biking trails that weave through the region's rugged landscapes. Here are some exhilarating options for mountain biking:

1. **Freiburg Bike Park:** Unleash your skills at the Freiburg Bike Park, a playground for mountain biking enthusiasts. The park features a variety of trails for all skill levels, including downhill and dirt jump courses.
2. **Schonach Mountain Bike Trail:** Conquer the Schonach Mountain Bike Trail, a challenging route that takes you through dense forests and offers thrilling descents. The varied terrain and technical sections make it a favorite among experienced riders.
3. **Baiersbronn Singletrack Trails:** Explore the Baiersbronn Singletrack Trails, a network of trails that wind through the lush forest landscapes. These trails offer a mix of flowy sections, technical challenges, and breathtaking views.

ESSENTIAL TIPS

1. **Choose the Right Route:** Select a cycling or mountain biking route that matches your skill level and experience.
2. **Gear Up:** Ensure your bike is in good condition and equip yourself with appropriate safety gear, including helmets and protective clothing.
3. **Stay Hydrated:** Carry ample water and stay hydrated throughout your ride, especially on warm days.
4. **Navigation Tools:** Bring along a map, GPS device, or smartphone app to navigate the trails effectively.
5. **Respect Nature:** Follow designated trails, respect wildlife, and adhere to Leave No Trace principles to preserve the natural beauty.
6. **Safety First:** Observe traffic rules and exercise caution when cycling on roads. Be mindful of pedestrians and other trail users.

Whether you're a leisure cyclist seeking scenic routes or an avid mountain biker craving thrilling descents, the Black Forest's cycling and mountain biking offerings cater to a wide range of preferences. With each rotation of the pedals, the region's natural splendor unveils itself in vibrant detail, inviting you to forge a deeper connection with its landscapes. So, gear up, saddle your trusty steed, and embark on an unforgettable journey through the captivating beauty of the Black Forest

WATER SPORTS ON STUNNING LAKES

In Black Forest, a symphony of lakes awaits, each offering a unique aquatic playground for water sports enthusiasts. Let's dive into the sparkling waters and explore the myriad lakes that grace this enchanting region, along with the exhilarating water sports they have to offer.

1. Lake Titisee: Where Dreams Sail

As the largest lake in the Black Forest, Lake Titisee is a haven for water sports aficionados:

Lake Titisee

- **Sailing:** Feel the wind in your sails as you navigate the pristine waters of Lake Titisee, surrounded by breathtaking scenery.
- **Swimming:** Take a refreshing plunge into the crystal-clear lake, reveling in the invigorating embrace of nature.
- **Paddleboarding:** Balance serenely atop the tranquil surface, paddle in hand, and soak in the serenity of this picturesque setting.
- **Canoeing and Kayaking:** Explore hidden coves and captivating shoreline, gliding through the waters in a canoe or kayak.

2. Schluchsee:

Schluchsee, the second-largest lake, invites adventure seekers to partake in heart-pounding activities:

Schluchsee

- **Windsurfing:** Harness the power of the wind to skim the water's surface, a thrilling experience amid stunning scenery.
- **Sailing:** Set sail on the expansive Schluchsee, where the breeze guides you through a landscape of natural beauty.

3. Feldsee:

Nestled amidst the mountains, Feldsee offers a peaceful respite and an opportunity for rowing enthusiasts:

- **Rowing:** Rent a rowboat and gently row across the serene expanse of Feldsee, embracing the solitude of this serene oasis.

4. Mummelsee:

Mummelsee, nestled in a magical setting, offers a tranquil escape for water lovers:

Mummelsee

- **Boating:** Embark on a leisurely boat ride across the shimmering surface of Mummelsee, surrounded by enchanting forests.

5. Schlüchtsee: Nature's Playground

Schlüchtsee beckons with a variety of water sports, inviting exploration of its pristine waters:

- **Swimming:** Immerse yourself in the refreshing waters of Schlüchtsee, framed by lush foliage and tranquil surroundings.
- **Kayaking:** Glide along the lake's edge in a kayak, exploring its hidden corners and embracing the serenity.

6. Nonnenmattweiher: A Hidden Gem

Discover the charm of Nonnenmattweiher, a hidden gem offering a serene space for relaxation and water activities:

- **Picnicking:** Enjoy a leisurely lakeside picnic with family and friends, savoring the idyllic atmosphere.

TIPS FOR A MEMORABLE EXPERIENCE

1. **Safety Gear:** Prioritize safety by wearing appropriate gear, such as life jackets, during water sports activities.
2. **Local Guidelines:** Familiarize yourself with local rules and regulations to ensure a responsible and respectful experience.
3. **Environmental Stewardship:** Preserve the natural beauty of the lakes by refraining from littering and respecting the ecosystem.
4. **Weather Awareness:** Stay informed about weather conditions to ensure a safe and enjoyable water sports experience.

From the majestic Lake Titisee to the hidden charms of Nonnenmattweiher, the lakes of the Black Forest offer a treasure trove of water sports opportunities. Whether you're seeking the thrill of windsurfing, the serenity of paddleboarding, or the simple joy of rowing, these aquatic playgrounds are ready to welcome you.

WILDLIFE WATCHING AND PHOTOGRAPHY

Venture into this natural sanctuary, where every rustling leaf and fleeting movement offers a chance to witness the region's diverse wildlife. Join us on a journey of wildlife watching and photography, as we unveil the enchanting inhabitants that call the Black Forest home.

1. Deer and Roe Deer:
   As you traverse the forest trails, keep an eye out for the elegant deer and roe deer that gracefully roam the woodlands. With their distinctive antlers and gentle presence, they are a sight to behold.

2. Foxes: Mystique of the Night
   The elusive foxes of the Black Forest often emerge under the cloak of night, their bright eyes gleaming in the darkness. With patience and a keen eye, you may catch a glimpse of these nocturnal wanderers.

3. Wild Boars:
   Venture into the heart of the forest to witness the sturdy and formidable wild boars. These sturdy creatures roam the undergrowth, adding an element of wilderness to the landscape.

4. Red Squirrels: Nature's Acrobats
   In the treetops, the nimble red squirrels put on a show of agility and acrobatics. Capture their playful antics as they navigate the branches and forage for food.

5. Birds of Beauty:
   The Black Forest resonates with the melodious tunes of its feathered residents:

- **Black Woodpecker:** Catch a glimpse of this striking bird as it taps rhythmically on the trees, a master of its craft.

- **European Robin:** The cheerful song of the European robin echoes through the forest, a harbinger of natural beauty.

6. Butterflies and Insects:
Pause to appreciate the intricate world of butterflies and insects:

- **Common Blue Butterfly:** A delicate visitor, the common blue butterfly graces the meadows with its ethereal presence.
- **Dragonflies:** Marvel at the aerial prowess of dragonflies as they dart and hover above the water's surface.

7. Owls: Guardians of the Night
The enigmatic owls of the Black Forest are elusive and captivating:

- **Tawny Owl:** Seek out the tawny owl, often seen at twilight, its haunting calls echoing through the forest.

8. Wild Cats: A Rare Glimpse
A symbol of the region's untamed beauty, the elusive wild cats occasionally make appearances in the Black Forest's depths.

Photography Tips for Capturing Nature's Essence

1. **Patience and Stillness:** Approach wildlife with patience, allowing them to become accustomed to your presence.
2. **Natural Light:** Leverage the soft, golden light of sunrise and sunset to capture the natural beauty of the animals.
3. **Camouflage and Stealth:** Blend into the surroundings and move slowly to avoid disturbing the creatures you wish to photograph.
4. **Respectful Distance:** Maintain a respectful distance to ensure both your safety and the animals' well-being.
5. **Zoom Lenses:** Utilize telephoto lenses to capture intricate details without getting too close.

CHAPTER 8

BUDGET-FRIENDLY ACTIVITIES

EXPLORING FREE AND LOW-COST ATTRACTIONS

T he allure of the Black Forest extends beyond its natural beauty, encompassing a world of affordable and captivating experiences. Join us as we unveil a trove of budget-friendly activities that allow you to immerse yourself in the region's charm without breaking the bank. From breathtaking vistas to cultural gems, these attractions offer a delightful blend of enrichment and affordability.

1. Forest Strolls: Nature's Bounty at No Cost

Embark on leisurely forest strolls that cost nothing but time and curiosity. Wander along well-maintained trails that wind through woodlands, offering glimpses of wildlife and serene landscapes. The tranquility of these walks is a balm for the soul, and the beauty of nature comes without a price tag.

2. Triberg Waterfalls: Nature's Grandeur for a Small Fee

Experience the majesty of the Triberg Waterfalls, where a nominal entrance fee grants you access to Germany's highest waterfalls. As the cascading water creates a symphony of sound, you'll find yourself surrounded by verdant foliage and breathtaking beauty.

3. Black Forest Open-Air Museum: A Glimpse into History

Step into the past at the Black Forest Open-Air Museum, where history comes alive in a charming village setting. For a modest admission fee, you can explore traditional farmhouses, workshops, and exhibits that paint a vivid picture of life in the region over the centuries.

4. Local Markets:

Peruse the stalls of local markets that offer a feast for the senses. From vibrant produce to artisan crafts, these markets are a treasure trove of authenticity. You can take in the sights, sounds, and scents of local life without spending much.

5. Historical Churches and Buildings: Stepping into the Past

Many historical churches and buildings in the Black Forest can be explored at little to no cost. Marvel at the architecture, intricate details, and centuries-old stories that these structures hold.

6. Lake Titisee and Schluchsee: Nature's Playground

Enjoy the beauty of Lake Titisee and Schluchsee without spending a fortune. Dip your toes in the clear waters, take a leisurely stroll along the shores, or simply bask in the peaceful ambiance that these lakes provide.

7. Picnics in Natural Settings: A Wallet-Friendly Feast

Pack a picnic and savor a meal surrounded by nature's beauty. Many parks, forests, and lakes in the Black Forest provide ideal spots for enjoying a budget-friendly feast.

8. Cultural Festivals and Events: Experiencing Tradition

Check the local event calendar for free or low-cost cultural festivals and events that celebrate the region's heritage. From music and dance to crafts and food, these gatherings offer an authentic glimpse into Black Forest culture.

Exploring the Black Forest on a budget need not compromise the quality of your experience. With careful planning and a spirit of adventure, you can discover the region's treasures without straining your wallet. Embrace the blend of nature, culture, and affordability that the Black Forest offers, creating memories that will last a lifetime.

AFFORDABLE LOCAL EATERIES

A culinary journey through the Black Forest doesn't have to strain your wallet. Join us as we delve into a delightful array of local eateries that offer savory flavors without the hefty price tag. From traditional favorites to international fare, these wallet-friendly dining options promise not only delectable dishes but also an unforgettable culinary experience.

1. Gasthäuser: Authentic Flavors at Affordable Prices
Gasthäuser, the heart of Black Forest dining, bring you authentic dishes without the high cost. Savor hearty stews, sausages, and schnitzels that capture the essence of the region. **Average meal price: €8-€15.**

2. Bäckereien: Bakery Delights for Every Palate
Local bakeries, or Bäckereien, offer freshly baked bread, pastries, and sandwiches at reasonable prices. Enjoy a quick, budget-friendly snack or a light meal. **Average price: €3-€8.**

3. Imbiss Stands: Quick Bites with Character
For a swift and satisfying meal on the go, visit Imbiss stands. Delight in bratwursts, currywursts, and other street food specialties. **Average price: €4-€6.**

4. Cafés: Affordable Brews and Bites
Black Forest cafés provide a cozy atmosphere for a budget-friendly experience. Sip locally roasted coffee with cake or a light sandwich. **Average price: €5-€10.**

5. Local Markets:

Explore local markets for fresh, affordable produce. Craft your own picnic with artisan cheeses, fruits, and bread from market stalls. **Average cost for a picnic: €10-€15.**

6. Food Trucks:

Keep an eye out for food trucks offering creative and pocket-friendly dishes. These mobile eateries often serve international cuisine with a unique twist. **Average price: €5-€8.**

7. Eateries Off the Beaten Path:

Venture beyond tourist hotspots to discover eateries beloved by locals. These hidden gems offer authentic meals at local-friendly prices. **Average price: €8-€12.**

8. Self-Catering:

Opt for self-catering by gathering ingredients from local markets or stores. Create your own picnic amidst the breathtaking Black Forest landscapes. **Average cost for picnic supplies: €10-€20.**

Indulging in the Black Forest's culinary scene doesn't have to strain your budget. Whether it's the warmth of Gasthäuser, the charm of Bäckereien, or the convenience of food trucks, you can experience the region's flavors without overspending. Each bite brings you closer to the heart of the Black Forest, creating cherished memories that won't cost a fortune.

Some tips for finding affordable local eateries in the Black Forest:

- **Ask locals for recommendations.** They will know the best places to eat that are both affordable and good.
- **Look for restaurants that are off the beaten path.** These restaurants are often less expensive than the ones in the tourist areas.
- **Check out the menus online before you go.** This will give you an idea of

the prices and what kind of food they serve.

· **Be flexible with your meal times.** Eating at off-peak times can save you money.

SELF-GUIDED WALKING TOURS

There's something enchanting about discovering a destination at your own pace, following winding trails that lead to hidden treasures and captivating sights. The Black Forest invites you to embark on a series of self-guided walking tours, each offering a unique perspective on its landscapes, history, and culture. Lace up your shoes and get ready to explore the region's riches step by step.

1. Triberg Waterfalls: Waterfall Walk

Begin your journey with a leisurely **2-kilometer** stroll along the path that winds beside the Triberg Waterfalls. As the highest waterfalls in Germany, they cascade down a total of **1,632 meters**, creating a mesmerizing spectacle. This 1-hour walk promises stunning views and the soothing sound of rushing water.

2. Titisee-Neustadt: Historical Walk

Step into the charm of Titisee-Neustadt on a **3-kilometer** historical walk that unveils the heart of this lakeside town. As you wander through its historic center, you'll encounter architectural gems and picturesque streets. The walk takes about 1.5 hours, allowing you to soak in the town's ambiance.

3. Furtwangen: Clock Museum Walk

Journey to Furtwangen for a **1-kilometer** walk that leads you to the renowned Black Forest Clock Museum. This museum is a testament to the region's clockmaking heritage. Spend around 30 minutes exploring the fascinating exhibits that reveal the intricacies of crafting these timekeeping marvels.

4. Belchen: Panorama Walk

Elevate your experience with a **5-kilometer** hike to the summit of Belchen, the second-highest peak in the Black Forest. This trail rewards you with panoramic vistas that stretch across the landscape. Allow approximately 2.5 hours to complete this invigorating hike, capturing breathtaking photos along the way.

5. Murgsee: Lakeside Walk

Indulge in the tranquility of a **4-kilometer** lakeside walk around the captivating Murgsee. With its serene ambiance and picturesque surroundings, this 1.5-hour stroll is perfect for immersing yourself in nature's beauty and capturing the essence of the region.

These self-guided walking tours offer a canvas on which you can paint your own Black Forest adventure. Whether you're drawn to cascading waterfalls, historic towns, clockmaking heritage, panoramic vistas, or serene lakes, there's a trail that speaks to your curiosity. Every step you take leads to discoveries that will forever remain etched in your memories of this remarkable destination. So, step forward, embrace the freedom of exploration, and let the Black Forest unfold its wonders before you.

CHAPTER 9

LOCAL CULTURE

UNDERSTANDING BLACK FOREST TRADITIONS

As you journey through the breathtaking landscapes of the Black Forest, you'll quickly realize that its allure extends far beyond its natural beauty. Nestled within its charming towns and villages are captivating traditions that have been cherished for generations. Let's take a deeper look into the tapestry of Black Forest culture and traditions, immersing ourselves in the essence of this enchanting region.

1. Cuckoo Clock Craftsmanship: A Time-Honored Tradition

At the heart of Black Forest culture is the exquisite craftsmanship of the cuckoo clock. These intricate timepieces are not just functional; they are works of art that reflect the region's creativity and precision. Dive into the world of clockmakers' studios and witness the dedication that goes into crafting these charming timekeepers. From traditional designs to modern interpretations, cuckoo clocks embody the essence of Black Forest ingenuity.

2. Woodcarving: Breathing Life into Timber

Black Forest woodcarving is a living testament to the region's artistic heritage. The skillful hands of artisans transform blocks of wood into intricate figurines, scenes, and ornaments that narrate stories of tradition and culture.

Whether it's adorable animals, mythical creatures, or nativity scenes, these hand-carved creations capture the essence of Black Forest life and creativity.

3. Traditional Attire:

The Black Forest's rich cultural tapestry is woven into its traditional attire. Adorned with vibrant colors and intricate patterns, these costumes offer a glimpse into the region's history and identity. From festivals to special occasions, locals proudly don these garments, breathing life into age-old traditions and celebrating the uniqueness of the Black Forest culture.

4. Local Cuisine:

No exploration of culture is complete without savoring the flavors of the land. Black Forest cuisine is a blend of hearty and flavorful dishes that reflect the region's agricultural heritage. Feast on specialties such as Black Forest ham, hearty stews, and the iconic Schwarzwälder Kirschtorte (Black Forest cake). These culinary delights not only satisfy the palate but also provide a window into the culinary traditions that have shaped the region.

5. Music and Dance:

Immerse yourself in the vibrant musical heritage of the Black Forest. From traditional folk tunes to lively dances, music is deeply ingrained in the local culture. Explore festivals where traditional music enlivens the air, and witness dance performances that celebrate the joy of life. The melodies and rhythms echo the spirit of the region, inviting you to join in the celebration.

6. Festivals and Celebrations:

Throughout the year, the Black Forest comes alive with festivals and celebrations that reflect its cultural vibrancy. From vibrant carnival processions to enchanting Christmas markets, these events offer a glimpse into the region's soul. Experience the merriment of local festivals, where the community gathers to honor age-old traditions, create cherished memories, and share the joy of being part of the Black Forest's rich tapestry.

7. Art and Craft Studios:

Wander through the workshops of local artisans, where age-old crafts continue to thrive. From glassblowing to pottery, these studios are a living testament to the enduring spirit of craftsmanship. Engage with artisans, learn about their techniques, and bring home handcrafted mementos that encapsulate the Black Forest's artistic prowess.

8. Traditional Folk Celebrations:

Dive into the realm of traditional folk celebrations that punctuate the Black Forest's calendar. From the exuberant Fastnacht Carnival to the enchanting Walpurgis Night, these festivities offer a glimpse into the region's playful spirit and ancient customs. Embrace the joy of costume parades, masked balls, and folklore, as you become a part of the vivacious traditions that define the Black Forest.

The traditions of the Black Forest are not just relics of the past; they are living expressions of the region's soul. As you immerse yourself in these cultural gems, you're not merely an observer—you become a participant in a legacy that has endured for centuries. By embracing Black Forest traditions, you gain a deeper connection to the people, the land, and the stories that have shaped this captivating corner of the world.

Here are some tips for experiencing Black Forest traditions:

- **Visit a museum:** There are many museums in the Black Forest that showcase the region's traditional crafts and culture.
- **Attend a festival:** There are many festivals held in the Black Forest throughout the year that celebrate the region's traditions.
- **Talk to locals:** The best way to learn about Black Forest traditions is to talk to the locals. They will be happy to share their stories and experiences with you.
- **Try traditional food:** There are many traditional Black Forest dishes that you can try, such as Spätzle, Black Forest ham, and Black Forest cake.

· **Buy souvenirs:** There are many traditional Black Forest souvenirs that you can buy, such as cuckoo clocks, woodcarvings, and Bollenhut hats.

FOLKLORE AND MYTHOLOGY

This is a realm where folklore and mythology dance in harmony, shaping the cultural identity of the region. Join us as we journey into the realm of Black Forest legends, where mythical creatures roam and ancient stories come to life.

1. The Lore of the Kobolds: Guardians of the Earth

Step into a world where mischievous spirits known as Kobolds dwell. These mystical beings are said to reside within the depths of the Black Forest, safeguarding its secrets. Often depicted as miners, they are believed to guide miners and protect the Earth's treasures. These playful spirits are a testament to the region's deep connection to its natural landscape.

2. The Wild Hunt: A Haunting Spectacle

Amidst the moonlit nights of the Black Forest, the echoes of the Wild Hunt reverberate. This spectral procession, led by a supernatural hunter, is said to sweep across the skies, foretelling doom or great change. As the wind rustles through the trees, the sound of galloping hooves is a reminder of the otherworldly forces that shape the destiny of the Black Forest.

3. The Legend of the Nibelungen: Epic Tales of Heroes

The Nibelungenlied, a medieval German epic, weaves together stories of heroes, dragons, and treasure. Within the Black Forest, this legend finds a home, as its heroes traverse the mystical landscape on quests of valor and discovery. The tale resonates through the region, offering a glimpse into the enduring power of myth to shape cultures and beliefs.

4. Black Forest Witches: Whispers of the Brocken

On the eve of Walpurgis Night, the Brocken Mountain beckons with whispers of witches and sorcery. This mystical gathering is said to be a time when witches from all corners of the land convene to dance and revel. The Brocken's shadowy silhouette against the moonlit sky becomes a canvas for tales of magic and mystery that have captivated the imaginations of generations.

5. Lake Titisee's Lady: A Watery Enigma

The tranquil waters of Lake Titisee hold a secret—a legend of an enchanting lady who emerges from the depths. Known as the "Titisee Woman," she is said to lure unsuspecting souls with her beauty, guiding them beneath the waters' surface. This haunting tale blends the ethereal with the eerie, a testament to the Black Forest's ability to infuse ordinary places with extraordinary stories.

6. Tales of Forest Spirits: Guardians of Nature

Within the heart of the Black Forest, nature's spirits are said to roam. From the elusive moss people to the protective tree spirits, these mythical creatures are the guardians of the forest's delicate balance. As you wander through ancient trees and tranquil clearings, you might catch a glimpse of these spirits, a reminder of the interconnectedness between folklore and nature.

7. The Echoes of Minstrels: Songs of Yore

From the depths of history, minstrels once sang ballads that carried the stories of heroes and legends. Their songs echoed through the valleys and forests, weaving tales of adventure and love. Though the minstrels have faded into history, their spirit lives on in the melodies that still resonate through the Black Forest, inviting you to be a part of its lyrical legacy.

TRADITIONAL MUSIC AND DANCE

Amidst the emerald embrace of the Black Forest, a symphony of traditional music and dance weaves a timeless melody that resonates with the region's cultural soul. Step into a world where every rhythm, every note, tells a story that stretches back through the annals of time. Join us as we explore the vibrant world of Black Forest music and dance, where heritage comes alive through sound and movement.

1. Polkas and Waltzes: Whirling Through Time

In the heart of the Black Forest, polkas and waltzes reverberate through the air, inviting you to join the dance. These lively and rhythmic tunes have been passed down through generations, offering a spirited glimpse into the region's joyous celebrations. As the accordion and fiddle play in harmony, you'll find yourself swept away by the infectious energy of the dance floor.

2. Schuhplattler: The Rhythmic Stamp of Tradition

The Schuhplattler is a dance that has deep roots in the Black Forest's folklore. This lively and rhythmic performance involves synchronized foot stomping, clapping, and intricate choreography. As the dancers move with precision and flair, the Schuhplattler becomes a vibrant portrayal of the region's heritage, connecting the present to the echoes of the past.

3. Yodeling: Echoes of the Mountains

As the mist rolls over the mountains, the haunting echoes of yodeling fill the air. This unique vocal technique, characterized by rapid changes between low and high pitches, is a cherished form of expression in the Black Forest. With each melodious yodel, you'll feel the connection to the mountains and valleys that have inspired this age-old tradition.

4. Zither and Accordion: Instruments of Tradition

The zither and accordion are the heartbeat of Black Forest music. With their soulful melodies, these instruments capture the essence of the region's landscapes and stories. Whether it's the melancholic strains of a zither or the lively tunes of an accordion, the music flows like a river, carrying with it the emotions and experiences of generations past.

5. Waltzing Through Time: The Elegance of Walzer

Among the rhythmic pulse of tradition, the waltz emerges as a graceful partner to history. Originating from Austria and Germany, this dance captures hearts with its flowing motions and timeless allure. Often gracing weddings and formal gatherings, the waltz is a celebration of unity and elegance. As couples glide across the floor, the waltz becomes a living embodiment of refined harmony.

6. Ländler: Vibrant Echoes of Bavaria

In the heart of the Black Forest's cultural mosaic, the Ländler dance takes center stage. With its vivacious and spirited movements, the Ländler shares a kinship with the waltz. Rooted in Bavarian traditions, this dance captures the essence of community and revelry. As dancers twirl and sway, the Ländler infuses the air with an infectious energy that transcends time.

7. Schwarzwaldlied: A Joyful Ode to Nature's Beauty

Amidst the jubilant gatherings of the Black Forest, the Schwarzwaldlied rings out like a cheerful proclamation. This traditional folk song, sung with exuberance, extols the splendor of the region's landscapes. With each spirited verse, the Schwarzwaldlied unites voices in a harmonious tribute to the captivating beauty that surrounds.

8. Bollenhut Dance: Graceful Elegance in Motion

As the sun sets over the Black Forest, the Bollenhut Dance comes to life with grace and artistry. Women don the iconic Bollenhüte, crowned with vibrant pompoms, and embark on a dance of elegance. With each step and twirl, this traditional dance evokes a sense of timelessness, preserving the finesse of generations past.

9. Jodel: Echoes Across the Mountains

Among the mountain peaks and wooded valleys, the art of jodeling resounds with heartfelt emotion. This distinctive form of singing, characterized by its swift shifts between chest voice and falsetto, serves as both a musical expression and a means of communication. As voices soar and echo, jodeling transcends barriers, connecting souls across vast landscapes.

10. Festivals and Celebrations: A Cultural Melting Pot

Throughout the year, the Black Forest comes alive with festivals and celebrations that showcase its musical heritage. From the Schwarzwald Musik Festival to the Donaueschingen Music Festival, these events provide a platform for both traditional and contemporary performances. The fusion of old and new creates a dynamic atmosphere that bridges the gap between generations.

As you immerse yourself in the world of Black Forest music and dance, you'll find that the region's cultural heartbeat continues to thrive. Local music schools, clubs, and workshops are dedicated to passing down these cherished traditions to future generations. Whether you're an eager learner or simply an appreciative listener, there's a place for you in this symphony of heritage.

The melodies and movements of Black Forest music and dance are more than just entertainment—they are a celebration of identity, a link to ancestors, and a bridge to the future. With each step of the dance and each note of the song, you become a part of the living legacy that harmonizes with the rhythms of tradition. So, whether you're tapping your feet to a polka, swaying to a waltz, or sharing in the joyous chorus of a Schwarzwaldlied, remember that in the Black Forest, the echoes of history find their voice in the music and dance of today.

CHAPTER 10

PLANNED ITINERARIES

WEEKEND GETAWAYS IN THE BLACK FOREST

E scape the hustle and bustle of daily life and immerse yourself in the tranquil embrace of the Black Forest. Whether you're seeking a romantic retreat, a nature-filled adventure, or a cultural exploration, the Black Forest offers a myriad of options for a memorable weekend getaway. Join us as we craft enchanting itineraries that will lead you through the heart of this captivating region, ensuring that your weekend escape is nothing short of extraordinary.

Itinerary 1: Romance Among the Pines

Day 1: Arrival in Romantic Triberg

- Check into a charming bed and breakfast nestled amidst the Black Forest's serenity.
- Explore the picturesque town of Triberg and visit the iconic Triberg Waterfalls.
- Dine at a cozy local restaurant, savoring Black Forest delicacies.

Day 2: Love and Leisure in Freiburg

- Embark on a scenic drive to Freiburg, the heart of the Black Forest.
- Stroll hand in hand through Freiburg's historic old town, admiring its medieval charm.
- Savor a romantic dinner at a local restaurant, accompanied by fine wine.

Day 3: Mountain Views and Starry Nights

- Ascend to Feldberg, the Black Forest's highest peak, and revel in panoramic vistas.
- Enjoy a leisurely hike amidst lush forests or take a cable car to the summit.
- Sip wine under the stars as you reflect on the enchanting moments of your weekend.

Itinerary 2: Nature's Embrace

Day 1: Exploring the Untamed Wilderness

- Arrive in Baiersbronn, a nature lover's haven, and settle into your cozy accommodation.
- Embark on a self-guided walking tour through the town's lush landscapes.
- Dine at a local eatery known for its farm-to-table cuisine.

Day 2: Hiking Adventures in the Heart of the Forest

- Journey to Schluchsee, where serene waters meet pristine woods.
- Choose from a variety of hiking trails, each offering a unique perspective of the area.
- Relax by the lakeshore, absorbing the tranquility that envelops you.

Day 3: A Journey Through Gorges and Valleys

- Depart for the captivating Wutachschlucht, a dramatic gorge carved by time.
- Trek through its rugged terrain, crossing bridges and taking in the

breathtaking views.
- Bid adieu to the Black Forest with a sense of accomplishment and renewal.

Itinerary 3: Cultural Immersion

Day 1: Arrival in Historic Gengenbach

- Settle into your accommodation in Gengenbach, a town rich in history and charm.
- Explore the cobbled streets, admiring the timber-framed architecture.
- Savor a traditional meal at a local tavern.

Day 2: Unveiling Black Forest Traditions

- Begin your day with a visit to the Black Forest Open-Air Museum in Gutach.
- Immerse yourself in the region's folklore, crafts, and heritage.
- Return to Gengenbach and join a guided tour to learn about the town's captivating past.

Day 3: A Glimpse of Fairy Tales

- Head to Triberg and visit the House of 1000 Clocks, a showcase of Black Forest craftsmanship.
- Take a leisurely stroll through the charming streets and enjoy a final taste of Black Forest cake.
- Depart with a newfound appreciation for the region's rich cultural tapestry.

FAMILY-FRIENDLY ADVENTURES

Embarking on a family getaway to the Black Forest promises to be an unforgettable experience filled with laughter, exploration, and cherished memories. With a diverse array of attractions and activities catering to all ages, the region offers the perfect playground for a family adventure. Join us as we unveil a delightful itinerary tailored to families seeking a harmonious blend of nature, culture, and fun.

Day 1: Welcome to Family Paradise
Arrival in Rust

- Check into a family-friendly hotel in Rust, a charming town near the Black Forest.
- Visit Europa-Park, one of Europe's most renowned theme parks, for an afternoon of exhilarating rides and attractions.

Day 2: A Day Amidst Natural Wonders
Triberg and Nature Exploration

- Embark on a scenic drive to Triberg and explore the Triberg Waterfalls.
- Enjoy a leisurely family hike along well-marked trails, discovering the beauty of the Black Forest's lush landscapes.

Day 3: Culture and Creativity
Freiburg and Creative Workshops

- Head to Freiburg and explore its vibrant old town.
- Engage in family-friendly workshops, such as pottery, painting, or cooking classes, to immerse yourselves in the local culture.

Day 4: Enchanting Encounters
Wildlife Park and Storytelling

- Visit the Black Forest Wildlife Park in Feldberg, where kids can get up close to native animals.
- Attend a traditional storytelling session in the park, allowing children to connect with local legends and folklore.

Day 5: Water Adventures

Lake Titisee and Water Activities

- Journey to Lake Titisee and spend the day by the water's edge.
- Engage in a range of water activities, from paddle boating and swimming to building sandcastles on the lakeshore.

Day 6: Chocolate Delight

Chocolate Museum and Culinary Adventure

- Explore the Hansel and Gretel-inspired Chocolate Museum in Walden-buch.
- Participate in a hands-on chocolate-making workshop, creating delectable treats as a family.

Day 7: Farewell with Fond Memories

Black Forest Railroad and Farewell

- Embark on a scenic ride aboard the Black Forest Railroad, a nostalgic journey through the region's picturesque landscapes.
- Bid farewell to the Black Forest, cherishing the memories you've created as a family.

NATURE LOVER'S RETREATS

For those seeking solace and rejuvenation amidst nature's embrace, the Black Forest beckons with its tranquil landscapes, lush forests, and serene vistas. This chapter invites nature enthusiasts to embark on a soul-soothing journey through some of the region's most idyllic retreats. Immerse yourself in the restorative power of the great outdoors as you follow this carefully curated itinerary designed to nourish the spirit and foster a deep connection with nature.

Day 1: Arrival and Forest Immersion
Check-In and Forest Bathing

- Arrive at your chosen accommodation nestled within the heart of the Black Forest.
- Indulge in a forest bathing session, allowing the healing energy of the woods to wash over you.

Day 2: Tranquil Trails and Meditative Walks
Explore the Kinzig Valley

- Embark on a serene hike through the Kinzig Valley, where ancient woodlands and meadows converge.
- Engage in mindful walking and embrace the meditative quality of your surroundings.

Day 3: Mountain Majesty and Reflection
Belchen Summit Hike

- Journey to the Belchen summit, one of the region's highest peaks.
- Savor the awe-inspiring panoramic views and find a peaceful spot for reflection.

Day 4: Waterside Bliss
Schluchsee Retreat

- Retreat to Schluchsee, a haven of serenity centered around the tranquil lake.
- Spend the day by the water's edge, practicing yoga or simply basking in the calm ambiance.

Day 5: Nature Connection and Creativity
Artistic Exploration

- Venture into the woods with your art supplies for a session of plein air painting.
- Let the beauty of the landscape inspire your creativity and forge a deeper connection to nature.

Day 6: Forest Silence and Starlit Skies
Silent Forest Walk and Stargazing

- Embark on a silent forest walk, allowing your senses to fully absorb the gentle sounds of nature.
- As night falls, enjoy a mesmerizing stargazing experience, with the Black Forest's clear skies revealing a celestial masterpiece.

Day 7: Farewell with Renewed Spirit
Morning Meditation and Farewell

- Begin your day with a guided meditation in nature, embracing the sense of renewal it brings.
- Bid farewell to the Black Forest, carrying with you the tranquility and vitality cultivated during your retreat.

This retreat offers more than a mere getaway; it provides a profound reconnection with the natural world and your inner self. Amidst the Black Forest's serene landscapes, you'll find respite from the hustle of everyday life and the opportunity to cultivate a deep sense of calm and contentment. Whether it's the quiet contemplation on a mountain summit or the gentle rustling of leaves during a forest walk, every moment in the Black Forest's embrace serves as a reminder of the innate harmony that exists between nature and the human soul.

CHAPTER 11

LANGUAGE AND COMMUNICATION

BASIC GERMAN PHRASES FOR TRAVELERS

While many locals speak English, showing an effort to communicate in their native language can create memorable connections and enhance your travel experience. This chapter introduces you to some basic German phrases that will prove invaluable during your time in the Black Forest, fostering interactions that go beyond mere transactions and transform into genuine exchanges.

Greetings and Common Courtesies:

- **Hello / Hi:** Hallo / Hi
- **Good morning:** Guten Morgen
- **Good afternoon:** Guten Tag
- **Good evening:** Guten Abend
- **Goodbye:** Auf Wiedersehen
- **Please:** Bitte
- **Thank you:** Danke
- **You're welcome:** Bitte schön
- **Excuse me / Sorry:** Entschuldigung

Introductions and Polite Inquiries:

- **My name is [Your Name]:** Ich heiße [Dein Name]
- **What is your name?:** Wie heißt du?
- **How are you?:** Wie geht es Ihnen? (formal) / Wie geht es dir? (informal)
- **I'm fine, thank you:** Mir geht es gut, danke
- **Where are you from?:** Woher kommst du?
- **I'm from [Your Country]:** Ich komme aus [Dein Land]

Navigating and Asking for Help:

- **Yes:** Ja
- **No:** Nein
- **Excuse me, where is [Place]?:** Entschuldigung, wo ist [Ort]?
- **I'm lost:** Ich habe mich verirrt
- **Can you help me?:** Können Sie mir helfen? (formal) / Kannst du mir helfen? (informal)

Dining and Ordering:

- **I would like [Item]:** Ich hätte gerne [Artikel]
- **How much does it cost?:** Wie viel kostet das?
- **The check, please:** Die Rechnung, bitte

Getting Around:

- **Where is the train station?:** Wo ist der Bahnhof?
- **Is this the right bus?:** Ist das der richtige Bus?
- **How much is a ticket to [Destination]?:** Wie viel kostet eine Fahrkarte nach [Ziel]?
- **Where can I buy a ticket?:** Wo kann ich eine Fahrkarte kaufen?

Emergencies:

- **Help!:** Hilfe!
- **I need a doctor:** Ich brauche einen Arzt
- **Police:** Polizei

Engaging with Local Culture:

- **Can you tell me about this?:** Können Sie mir davon erzählen?
- **I'm interested in learning more:** Ich interessiere mich dafür, mehr zu erfahren
- **What is this called?:** Wie nennt man das?

Remember, your efforts to speak German, even if it's just a few words, will be appreciated by the locals and can lead to meaningful interactions. Don't be afraid to try, and enjoy the enriching experience of connecting with the culture and people of the Black Forest through language.

NAVIGATING LANGUAGE BARRIERS

As you explore the captivating landscapes and cultural treasures of the Black Forest, you might encounter situations where language barriers create a temporary challenge in communication. Fear not, for with a little creativity, patience, and understanding, you can navigate these hurdles and make the most of your experience. This chapter offers practical tips and strategies to help you communicate effectively, even when faced with language differences.

1. **Learn Basic Phrases:** Familiarize yourself with essential phrases in the local language, such as greetings, polite inquiries, and expressions of gratitude. Even a few words can go a long way in showing respect and making connections.

2. **Use Visual Aids:** A picture is worth a thousand words. Utilize images, gestures, and non-verbal cues to convey your needs or ask for directions.

Pointing to a map, miming actions, or using hand signals can bridge gaps in communication.

3. Utilize Translation Apps: Technology can be your ally. Download translation apps that allow you to input text or even use the camera to translate signs, menus, and written text in real-time.

4. Carry a Phrasebook: Bring along a pocket-sized phrasebook with translations of common phrases and words. It can be a quick reference when faced with unfamiliar situations.

5. Write It Down: If you're struggling to communicate verbally, consider writing down your questions or requests. Keep a small notebook and pen handy for this purpose.

6. Use Simple Language: When attempting to communicate, use simple sentences and avoid complex vocabulary. Speaking slowly and clearly can also enhance understanding.

7. Seek Assistance: Don't hesitate to ask for help from bilingual individuals, whether they are locals, fellow travelers, or service staff. They might be able to bridge the communication gap for you.

8. Be Patient and Respectful: Keep in mind that not everyone you encounter will speak your language. Be patient, maintain a friendly demeanor, and approach the situation with respect.

9. Smile and Express Gratitude: A genuine smile and a nod of gratitude can convey goodwill and appreciation, even when words are limited.

10. Embrace the Adventure: Embracing the challenge of navigating language barriers can be a memorable part of your travel experience. It's an opportunity to connect with locals on a different level and learn more about their culture.

Remember that the goal is to foster meaningful connections and mutual understanding. With a positive attitude and a willingness to adapt, you can successfully navigate language barriers and create memorable interactions during your journey through the Black Forest.

CHAPTER 12

PRACTICAL INFORMATION

CURRENCY AND MONEY MATTERS

As you journey through the Black Forest, it's important to be well-prepared when it comes to currency and money matters. Navigating the financial aspects of your trip can enhance your experience and ensure a seamless adventure. In this chapter, we'll look into key insights to help you manage your finances effectively while immersing yourself in the beauty of this picturesque region.

1. Currency: The official currency used in Germany is the Euro (€). This unit of currency is further divided into cents. Familiarize yourself with the appearance of Euro banknotes and coins to make transactions smoother.

2. Cash and Cards: While credit and debit cards are widely accepted in tourist areas, it's advisable to carry some cash for smaller establishments or remote areas. ATMs are readily available in towns and cities, allowing you to withdraw cash in Euros.

3. Currency Exchange: Currency exchange services can be found at airports, major train stations, and city centers. It's prudent to compare exchange rates and fees to ensure you get the best deal.

4. Banking Hours: German banks typically operate from Monday to Friday, with varying opening hours. Larger cities may have branches that offer extended hours, while smaller towns might close earlier.

5. Credit and Debit Cards: Major international credit and debit cards such as Visa and MasterCard are widely accepted. However, it's wise to carry a backup card and some cash in case you encounter places that prefer traditional payment methods.

6. Tipping Etiquette: Tipping is a common practice in Germany, though it's not mandatory. In restaurants, rounding up the bill or leaving a 5-10% tip is appreciated. Tipping for exceptional service is a thoughtful gesture.

7. Tax-Free Shopping: Non-European Union (EU) residents can often claim a refund on Value Added Tax (VAT) for certain purchases. Look for shops displaying the Tax-Free Shopping logo and inquire about the process at the point of purchase.

8. Budget Wisely: Before your trip, establish a budget that covers expenses like accommodations, meals, transportation, and activities. This will help you manage your finances and make the most of your experience.

9. Online Banking: Consider setting up online banking if your bank offers this service. It can be helpful for monitoring your account, checking transactions, and managing your funds while abroad.

10. Emergencies: Keep emergency contact information for your bank and credit card company in case you encounter any issues with your cards while traveling.

By staying informed and proactive in managing your finances, you can fully embrace the wonders of the Black Forest while ensuring a worry-free and enjoyable adventure.

BANKS IN BLACK FOREST

When traveling in the Black Forest, it's essential to have access to banking services. Here are some of the banks in the region, along with their branch locations and operation hours:

Volksbank Mittlerer Schwarzwald
   Branches: Many towns and villages in the Black Forest **Operation Hours:**

   · Monday to Friday: 8:30 am to 12:30 pm, 2:00 pm to 4:00 pm
   · Saturday: 9:00 am to 12:00 pm

Sparkasse Schwarzwald-Baar
   Branches: Many towns and villages in the Black Forest **Operation Hours:**

   · Monday to Friday: 8:30 am to 12:30 pm, 2:00 pm to 4:00 pm
   · Saturday: 9:00 am to 12:00 pm

Commerzbank
   Branches: larger towns in the Black Forest Operation Hours:

   · Monday to Friday: 9:00 am to 12:30 pm, 2:00 pm to 4:00 pm
   · Thursday: 9:00 am to 7:00 pm

Deutsche Bank
   Branches: Some larger towns in the Black Forest
   Operation Hours:

   · Monday to Friday: 9:00 am to 5:00 pm
   · Saturday: 9:00 am to 12:00 pm

Postbank
   Branches: Some larger towns in the Black Forest

Operation Hours:

· Monday to Friday: 9:00 am to 6:00 pm
· Saturday: 9:00 am to 1:00 pm

HypoVereinsbank
Branches: Some larger towns in the Black Forest
Operation Hours:

· Monday to Friday: 9:00 am to 5:00 pm
· Saturday: 9:00 am to 12:00 pm

DKB
Branches: Some larger towns in the Black Forest
Operation Hours:

· Monday to Friday: 9:00 am to 4:00 pm
· Saturday: 9:00 am to 12:00 pm

GLS Bank
Branch: Freiburg im Breisgau **Operation Hours:**

· Monday to Friday: 9:00 am to 5:00 pm
· Saturday: 9:00 am to 12:00 pm

Raiffeisenbank
Branches: Many towns and villages in the Black Forest **Operation Hours:**

· Monday to Friday: 8:30 am to 12:30 pm, 2:00 pm to 4:00 pm
· Saturday: 9:00 am to 12:00 pm

EMERGENCY CONTACTS AND SERVICES

- **Police:** 110
- **Fire department:** 112
- **Ambulance:** 112
- **Tourist information:** 0049 7652 910180
- **Roadside assistance:** ADAC: 0049 89 22222222
- **German Red Cross:** 0049 800 411 7711

You can also call 112 for all emergency services.

HOSPITALS AND CLINICS IN BLACK FOREST

When it comes to your health and well-being, having access to medical facilities is crucial. Here are some hospitals and clinics in the Black Forest, along with their locations and round-the-clock operation hours:

HOSPITALS

1. **Freiburg University Hospital:** The largest hospital in the Black Forest, located in Freiburg im Breisgau.
2. **Operation Hours:** 24/7
3. *Address:* Hugstetter Str. 49, 79106 Freiburg im Breisgau
4. **Klinikum Mittelbaden:** Situated in Offenburg, this hospital provides comprehensive medical services.
5. **Operation Hours:** 24/7
6. *Address:* Ebertplatz 12, 77654 Offenburg
7. **Sana Klinikum Offenburg:** Another medical center in Offenburg offering round-the-clock services.
8. **Operation Hours:** 24/7
9. *Address:* Weingartenstraße 70, 77654 Offenburg
10. **Helios Klinikum Bad Wildbad:** Located in Bad Wildbad, providing

continuous medical care.

11. **Operation Hours:** 24/7
12. *Address:* Katharinenstraße 1, 75323 Bad Wildbad
13. **Schwarzwald-Baar Klinikum Villingen-Schwenningen:** Found in Villingen-Schwenningen, this hospital offers 24/7 services.
14. **Operation Hours:** 24/7
15. *Address:* Röntgenstraße 1, 78052 Villingen-Schwenningen

Additional Hospitals and Clinics

1. **Klinikum Hochrhein:** Serving Waldshut-Tiengen, ensuring medical care around the clock.
2. **Operation Hours:** 24/7
3. *Address:* Spitalstraße 5, 79761 Waldshut-Tiengen
4. **Helios Klinikum Haslach:** Located in Haslach im Kinzigtal, offering 24/7 medical assistance.
5. **Operation Hours:** 24/7
6. *Address:* Theodor-Kaufmann-Platz 2, 77716 Haslach im Kinzigtal
7. **Klinikum St. Elisabeth:** Serving Ravensburg with continuous medical support.
8. **Operation Hours:** 24/7
9. *Address:* Elisabethenstraße 15, 88212 Ravensburg
10. **MediClin Klinik Herbolzheim:** Ensuring medical care round-the-clock in Herbolzheim.
11. **Operation Hours:** 24/7
12. *Address:* Am Eichenweg 1, 79336 Herbolzheim
13. **RKH Klinikum Mittlerer Oberrhein:** Located in Kehl, providing 24/7 medical services.
14. **Operation Hours:** 24/7
15. *Address:* Bürgerhospital, Großherzog-Friedrich-Straße 20, 77694 Kehl

Please remember that while these are some of the available medical facilities in the Black Forest, the specifics of operation hours and services may vary.

In case of a medical emergency, visiting the nearest hospital is crucial. Have important medical information and documents readily available for your visit. Stay safe and prioritize your well-being during your time in the Black Forest.

SAFETY TIPS FOR TRAVELERS

Ensuring your safety while exploring the captivating landscapes and charming towns of the Black Forest is essential. Here are some safety tips to keep in mind during your journey:

1. **Stay Informed:** Familiarize yourself with the local emergency numbers and the location of the nearest hospitals and police stations. This knowledge can be invaluable in case of any unforeseen circumstances.
2. **Health Precautions:** Prior to your trip, consult your healthcare provider about vaccinations and health recommendations for the region. Carry any necessary medications and prescriptions with you.
3. **Weather Awareness:** The weather in the Black Forest can vary, so check the forecast before heading out. Be prepared for sudden changes in weather and dress accordingly, especially if you plan to engage in outdoor activities.
4. **Hiking and Trekking:** If you're planning to hike or trek, choose trails that match your fitness level and experience. Carry essentials like water, snacks, a map, and a charged mobile phone. Inform someone about your route and estimated return time.
5. **Wildlife Interaction:** The Black Forest is home to diverse wildlife. Observe animals from a safe distance and avoid feeding them. If you encounter larger animals, like deer or wild boars, give them space to retreat.
6. **Driving Safety:** If you're renting a car, adhere to traffic rules and exercise caution on winding roads. Drive at a moderate speed, especially in foggy or rainy conditions.
7. **Language Basics:** While many locals may speak English, learning a few

basic German phrases can help you communicate effectively, especially in remote areas.

8. **Currency and Valuables:** Keep your valuables secure, either in a hotel safe or a concealed pouch. Carry a copy of important documents like your passport and ID.

9. **Outdoor Activities:** When participating in water sports, follow safety guidelines and wear life jackets. For hiking and biking, choose marked trails and inform someone about your plans.

10. **Local Customs:** Respect local customs and traditions. Dress appropriately when visiting churches or attending cultural events.

11. **Emergency Contacts:** Keep a list of emergency contacts handy, including your country's embassy or consulate.

12. **Local Advice:** If you're uncertain about a certain area or activity, seek advice from locals or tour operators. They can provide insights that enhance your safety.

13. **Travel Insurance:** Consider purchasing travel insurance that covers medical emergencies, trip cancellations, and unexpected incidents.

14. **COVID-19 Safety:** Stay updated on the latest COVID-19 guidelines and regulations. Adhere to mask-wearing and social distancing rules when required.

By following these safety tips, you can make the most of your experience in the Black Forest while ensuring your well-being and peace of mind. Enjoy your journey and embrace the beauty and culture of this enchanting region.

CHAPTER 13

TRAVELER'S CHECKLIST

PACKING ESSENTIALS

Preparing for your journey to the enchanting Black Forest requires careful packing to ensure you have everything you need for a memorable and comfortable trip. Here's a comprehensive checklist of essentials to consider:

CLOTHING AND ACCESSORIES:

- Comfortable walking shoes or hiking boots
- Lightweight, moisture-wicking clothing for layering
- Rainproof jacket or poncho
- Warm layers for cooler evenings
- Swimsuit and towel for lakes and water activities
- Sun hat or cap
- Sunglasses with UV protection
- Travel-friendly backpack or daypack
- Travel umbrella

PERSONAL ITEMS:

- Passport, ID, and copies of important documents
- Visa and travel insurance information
- Prescription medications and any necessary medical supplies
- Personal toiletries (toothbrush, toothpaste, shampoo, etc.)
- Sunscreen and insect repellent
- Personal hygiene items (wet wipes, hand sanitizer)
- First aid kit
- Contact lens solution and spare glasses

ELECTRONICS AND GADGETS:

- Mobile phone and charger
- Universal power adapter
- Portable charger or power bank
- Camera or smartphone for capturing memories
- Travel alarm clock or watch

TRAVEL DOCUMENTS AND FINANCES:

- Printed copies of your travel itinerary and accommodation reservations
- Credit and debit cards
- Cash in local currency
- Travel insurance information
- International driver's license (if renting a vehicle)
- Emergency contact list

OUTDOOR ADVENTURE GEAR:

- Hiking or trekking gear (if planning outdoor activities)
- Water-resistant backpack or dry bag for hiking
- Binoculars for wildlife observation
- Pocket knife or multi-tool

MISCELLANEOUS:

- Travel pillow and eye mask for comfortable rest
- Lightweight and quick-drying travel towel
- Language guidebook or translation app
- Notepad and pen for jotting down notes
- Snacks for on-the-go energy
- Reusable water bottle
- Ziplock bags for storing small items

OPTIONAL ITEMS:

- Travel journal or sketchbook
- Reading material or e-reader
- Portable travel pillow or cushion
- Snorkeling gear for lake exploration
- Travel laundry detergent for longer stays

As you pack, remember to consider the weather and the specific activities you plan to engage in. Keep in mind that packing light and versatile items will help you navigate your journey with ease. Adapt this checklist to your personal needs and preferences to ensure a seamless and enjoyable experience in the breathtaking landscapes of the Black Forest.

MUST-HAVE GEAR FOR OUTDOOR ACTIVITIES

Exploring the natural beauty of the Black Forest demands proper gear to ensure your safety, comfort, and enjoyment. Whether you're embarking on a challenging hike, a serene nature walk, or a thrilling bike ride, having the right equipment is essential. Here's a list of must-have gear to make the most of your outdoor adventures:

HIKING ESSENTIALS:

- **Sturdy Hiking Boots:** Invest in high-quality hiking boots that provide ankle support and comfort, especially for longer trails.
- **Appropriate Clothing:** Wear moisture-wicking clothing for layering, including a lightweight, long-sleeved shirt, hiking pants, and a rainproof jacket.
- **Backpack:** A durable and comfortable backpack is essential for carrying essentials like water, snacks, a first aid kit, and a map.
- **Navigation Tools:** Bring a map, compass, or GPS device to navigate trails confidently.
- **Water and Snacks:** Carry a reusable water bottle and energy-boosting snacks to stay hydrated and fueled.

BIKING NECESSITIES:

- **Mountain Bike or Hybrid Bike:** Choose a bike suited to the terrain you'll be covering, and ensure it's in good working condition.
- **Biking Helmet:** Protect your head with a well-fitting, certified biking helmet.
- **Biking Gloves:** Gloves offer grip, cushioning, and protection during long rides.
- **Repair Kit:** Pack a basic bike repair kit with tools, a spare tube, and a pump.
- **Apparel:** Wear moisture-wicking clothing, padded biking shorts, and appropriate shoes for efficient pedaling.

WATER ACTIVITIES GEAR:

- **Swimsuit:** A swimsuit is essential for swimming, kayaking, or other water sports in the lakes.
- **Quick-Drying Towel:** Opt for a lightweight, quick-drying towel to dry off after water activities.

- **Water Shoes:** Comfortable water shoes protect your feet while navigating rocky lake shores.
- **Sun Protection:** Pack waterproof sunscreen and a wide-brimmed hat to shield yourself from the sun.

GENERAL OUTDOOR EQUIPMENT:

- **First Aid Kit:** Ensure it includes bandages, antiseptic wipes, pain relievers, and any necessary personal medications.
- **Multi-Tool:** A versatile tool with pliers, a knife, screwdrivers, and more can be handy in various situations.
- **Flashlight or Headlamp:** Illuminate trails, campsites, or your surroundings in low-light conditions.
- **Insect Repellent:** Protect yourself from insects and ticks with effective repellents.
- **Portable Charger:** Keep your electronic devices powered for navigation or emergencies.

Remember that the gear you select should match the activities you plan and the specific conditions of the Black Forest. Safety is paramount, so make sure to inform others about your plans, stick to marked trails, and follow any park rules and regulations. With the right gear, you can fully embrace the Black Forest's outdoor splendor and create lasting memories.

PRE-TRIP TO-DO LIST

Planning a trip to the Black Forest requires careful preparation to ensure a smooth and enjoyable experience. Here's a comprehensive pre-trip checklist to help you cover all the essential details before embarking on your journey:

RESEARCH AND PLANNING:

- **Choose Travel Dates:** Determine the dates of your trip and consider the weather, local events, and peak tourist seasons.
- **Create Itinerary:** Plan your daily activities, including attractions, hikes, and leisure time.
- **Accommodation:** Book accommodations in advance, whether hotels, guesthouses, or vacation rentals.
- **Transportation:** Arrange transportation to and within the Black Forest, whether by car, train, or plane.

ESSENTIAL DOCUMENTS:

- **Passport and Visa:** Ensure your passport is valid and check if you need a visa for your nationality.
- **Identification:** Carry a photocopy of your passport and any necessary identification cards.
- **Travel Insurance:** Purchase comprehensive travel insurance covering health, accidents, and trip cancellations.

HEALTH AND SAFETY:

- **Vaccinations:** Check if any vaccinations are required for your destination.
- **Medications:** Pack any prescription medications you need and carry a copy of the prescription.
- **First Aid Kit:** Assemble a basic first aid kit with bandages, pain relievers, and other essentials.
- **Emergency Contacts:** Note down local emergency numbers, your country's embassy contact, and your accommodation's contact information.

FINANCES:

- **Currency:** Familiarize yourself with the local currency and consider bringing some cash for smaller expenses.
- **ATM Cards:** Check if your ATM card works internationally and notify your

bank about your travel dates.

· **Credit Cards:** Inform your credit card company about your travel plans to avoid any issues with transactions.

PACKING:

· **Clothing:** Pack weather-appropriate clothing, including comfortable walking shoes, rain gear, and warm layers.
· **Outdoor Gear:** Depending on your planned activities, pack gear like hiking boots, biking gloves, or swimwear.
· **Electronics:** Bring chargers, power banks, and any electronics you'll need for navigation or entertainment.
· **Personal Items:** Don't forget essentials like toiletries, sunscreen, and any personal comfort items.

COMMUNICATION:

· **Language:** Familiarize yourself with basic German phrases and consider a translation app.
· **Navigation:** Download offline maps and navigation apps for easy exploration.

MISCELLANEOUS:

· **Notify Loved Ones:** Share your travel plans with family or friends and keep them updated.
· **Unplug Appliances:** Ensure you unplug appliances and lock doors before leaving home.
· **Pets and Plants:** Make arrangements for the care of your pets and plants while you're away.

By ticking off these items on your pre-trip checklist, you'll set the stage for a well-prepared and unforgettable adventure in the enchanting Black Forest.

Safe travels and enjoy every moment of your journey!

CHAPTER 14

SUSTAINABILITY AND RESPONSIBLE TRAVEL

SUPPORTING LOCAL CONSERVATION EFFORTS

When visiting the stunning landscapes and cultural treasures of the Black Forest, it's important to embrace responsible travel practices that contribute to the preservation of its natural beauty and cultural heritage. By supporting local conservation efforts, you can leave a positive impact on the environment and the communities you visit. Here are some ways to be a responsible traveler in the Black Forest:

RESPECT NATURE:

- **Stay on Trails:** Stick to designated trails and paths to prevent erosion and protect delicate ecosystems.
- **Avoid Wildlife Disturbance:** Observe animals from a distance and refrain from feeding or getting too close to them.
- **Reduce Waste:** Pack reusable water bottles, utensils, and bags to minimize plastic waste.

CONTRIBUTE TO THE COMMUNITY:

- **Support Local Businesses:** Shop at local markets, eat at family-owned eateries, and purchase handmade crafts to bolster the local economy.

· **Respect Cultural Sites:** Treat historical and cultural sites with care, avoiding littering or vandalizing.

MINIMIZE YOUR FOOTPRINT:

· **Use Public Transportation:** Opt for public transportation or shared rides to reduce your carbon footprint.
· **Conserve Water and Energy:** Practice water and energy conservation in accommodations.

ENGAGE IN SUSTAINABLE ACTIVITIES:

· **Volunteer:** Consider participating in local conservation projects or community initiatives during your visit.
· **Eco-Friendly Accommodations:** Choose accommodations that have sustainability initiatives in place.

SUPPORT CONSERVATION ORGANIZATIONS:

· **Donate:** Research and donate to local organizations that focus on environmental conservation and cultural preservation.
· **Participate in Tours:** Choose eco-friendly tours that promote responsible wildlife viewing and support conservation efforts.

CULTURAL SENSITIVITY:

· **Learn Local Customs:** Familiarize yourself with local customs, traditions, and etiquette to show respect to the culture
· **Respect Photography Rules:** Ask permission before taking photos of people or sensitive cultural sites.

By embracing these sustainable travel practices, you can contribute to the preservation of the Black Forest's natural wonders and cultural treasures for generations to come. Your responsible choices help ensure that this beautiful region remains a thriving destination for both travelers and locals alike.

ECO-FRIENDLY TRAVEL PRACTICES

Adopting eco-friendly travel practices can make a significant difference in preserving the region's natural beauty and minimizing your environmental impact. Here are some tips for practicing sustainability during your travels in the Black Forest:

TRANSPORTATION:

- **Use Public Transportation:** The Black Forest has an efficient public transportation network. Opt for buses, trains, and trams to explore the region without contributing to traffic congestion and pollution.
- **Carpooling and Bike Rentals:** Consider carpooling or renting bicycles for shorter trips. Cycling is a wonderful way to immerse yourself in nature while reducing carbon emissions.

ACCOMMODATIONS:

- **Choose Eco-Friendly Lodging:** Look for accommodations that prioritize sustainability by conserving water, using renewable energy sources, and implementing recycling programs.
- **Reduce Energy Consumption:** When you leave your room, turn off lights, air conditioning, and electronics to conserve energy.

WASTE REDUCTION:

- **Pack Reusable Items:** Carry a reusable water bottle, shopping bag, and travel utensils to reduce the need for single-use plastics.

- **Minimize Packaging:** Purchase products with minimal packaging and avoid disposable items whenever possible.

RESPONSIBLE SIGHTSEEING:

- **Stick to Designated Trails:** Stay on marked paths to protect fragile ecosystems and avoid disturbing wildlife habitats.
- **Respect Wildlife:** Observe animals from a distance and avoid feeding them. Your presence should have minimal impact on their behavior.

LOCAL CUISINE:

- **Support Sustainable Dining:** Opt for eateries that source ingredients locally and promote sustainable practices.
- **Minimize Food Waste:** Order only what you can finish to avoid food waste. Consider taking leftovers with you if the option is available.

CULTURAL SENSITIVITY:

- **Learn Local Customs:** Familiarize yourself with local customs, traditions, and etiquette to engage respectfully with the culture.
- **Respect Cultural Sites:** Treat historical and cultural sites with care. Avoid touching artifacts and follow posted rules.

LEAVE NO TRACE:

- **Pack Out What You Bring In:** Dispose of waste properly and leave natural areas as you found them.
- **Collect Memories, Not Souvenirs:** Consider choosing sustainable souvenirs or experiences over mass-produced items.

If you adopting these eco-friendly travel practices, you can be a responsible and conscious traveler, making a positive impact on the Black Forest's environment and communities. Your efforts contribute to the region's long-term sustainability and ensure that its treasures are enjoyed by future generations.

Conclusion

As we reach the end of our guide, I want you to take a moment and imagine yourself standing amidst the serene beauty of the Black Forest. The whispering leaves, the gentle rustling of the trees, the melodic notes of traditional music – all of these elements combine to create a symphony of enchantment that will accompany you on your journey.

Throughout this guide, we've journeyed together, uncovering the hidden treasures and vibrant experiences that the Black Forest has to offer. From the majestic Triberg Waterfalls to the intricate dance of the Bollenhut, from the bustling markets to the tranquil lakeshores – each moment in this magical land has been crafted to fill your heart with wonder.

As you gear up for your adventure, imagine yourself setting foot on the trails, breathing in the crisp forest air, and letting the rich culture of the Black Forest seep into your being. Whether you're wandering through charming villages, delving into folklore, or immersing yourself in outdoor activities, know that every step you take will be guided by the spirit of exploration and discovery.

Picture yourself savoring the delectable flavors of local cuisine, capturing the beauty of the landscape through your lens, and creating memories that will be etched in your heart forever. The Black Forest isn't just a destination – it's an invitation to connect with nature, immerse yourself in culture, and find a sense of peace that only this enchanting region can provide.

As you embark on your adventure, remember that you're not just a traveler; you're a part of a legacy that spans generations. Your presence contributes to the sustainability and conservation of this cherished land, ensuring that its magic endures for years to come.

So pack your bags with excitement and curiosity, set forth on your journey, and let the Black Forest weave its spell around you. As you explore its trails, interact with its people, and relish its flavors, may you find a profound sense of joy and fulfillment that only travel can bring. Safe travels, fellow explorer, and may your time in the Black Forest be a chapter in your story that you'll treasure forever.

SAFE TRAVELS!!!
FROM THE
GERMAN SCHWARZWALD

Printed in Great Britain
by Amazon

38359972R00086